Contents.

Early days. Page 2.
Why did we win so many races. Page 35.
The Tracks. Page 43.
A Tale of two brood bitches. Page 46.
Changes & Parvovirus. Page 120.
Big Changes a coming. Page 137.
Stud dogs. Page 140.
Michael Dunne. Page 177.
Trendy Leigh (Brett Lee's brother). Page 183.
Litter brothers at stud. Page 189.
Finland. Page 190.
Changes in the game. Page 190.
Skillnets 2007. Page 197.
Good times & bad. Page 200.
Thoughts & Opinions. Page 225.
Postscript. Page 243.
Appendix A. Cost effective breeding. Page 246.

I have been involved with greyhounds most of my life in some form or another, adding up to over 30 years of direct involvement. I grew up in Northern Ireland at the height of the troubles in the '70s and '80s. My Da always had a couple of greys at the bottom of the garden in our council house in Antrim town and later in Belfast. So as far back as I can remember there was always a greyhound or two knocking about in my formative years. I recall going to collect the Sporting Press newspaper from a shop in Belfast city centre at seven years of age on my own one morning, which involved me getting a black taxi to and from the shop. This would be unthinkable today to send a seven-year-old on an errand like this, but I was always big for my age and acted older. Plus, I'd done this journey every week with my Da since I was a toddler, so he had no doubts I could do it. I couldn't see my seven-year-old son doing this today and I certainly wouldn't allow it.

I can remember some things well from this early period; despite the memories being over forty years old. My Da was friendly with a school teacher called Gerry Gorman who lived in Stoneyford, which is a rural area about six miles from Belfast. Gerry, who taught in the Christian Brothers Secondary school on the Glen Road in the city, was a greyhound enthusiast who had land and kennels. My Da later kept his dogs at Gerry's place and we used to spend a lot of summer evenings and weekend time there all year round. I don't know if my Da paid him for the use of his kennels or why they lost touch in the years to follow. I was very young at this time, but remember Gerry playing football with me, and my Da telling me Gerry had been a professional footballer who had played with Toronto Blizzards in Canada. After this period, I remember we had several pups reared with Joe Farmer near Keady in Armagh and went down every Sunday to see them. I remember we'd always take them out of the paddock they were in and let them gallop freely in an open field. Joe Farmer was known to have reared many champion dogs including 'Make History' the 1988 Irish Derby champ. I can't remember much about specific dogs of this period or how these pups turned out, but I can remember loving the conversations about dogs that I'd hear my Da and others having, soaking it up like a big sponge. There was another man by the name of John Mahon who lived in Portaferry; he and my Da had dogs in partnership. He had a small amount of land too and I remember visiting his place on certain Sundays, which necessitated getting the ferry from Strangford lough. These memories are very dim, but I recall him having young kids and we always had tea in their happy home after we'd seen the dogs. When any of the pups were reared, my Da would then take them home and start training them.

Of the dogs, I remember as a child, there was a dog called Fighting Mac my Da bought as a sapling along with a litter brother that turned out to be not much good. Fighting Mac was by Mic Mac who had been a decent staying type dog by Monalee Champion. I don't know any more details on the breeding, but these pups were born in Northern Ireland and were very reasonable as regards to purchase price or my Da wouldn't have bought them as he hadn't much money at this time. Fighting Mac (such a poor name for a genuine dog) caught his first hare at six months and became a fantastic catcher of hares in the brief time we owned him. We lived in a housing complex at the time in Rathinraw, which was a new, sprawling council estate at the time on the outskirts of Antrim town. In those days, the area was sparsely built up and there were fields galore all around the estate. One thing I got an appreciation for with dogs from my Da was giving them plenty of free running all year round and Fighting Mac, or Dusty as he was known to us, had a knack for catching hares that I've not seen the like of since by any other greyhound. The fields around Antrim at this time were rampant with hares and foxes. Nowadays, of course, hunting hares is illegal, but even today if you're exercising your dogs and they put a hare up, what can you do? They're going to give chase as they're doing what they're bred for and it's not as if anyone can accuse you of organised hunting. Very few greyhounds develop the knack for catching hares. Partly, this is due to most of the fields in Ireland being too small and tight with multiple hedging around them that allows the hare to slip away much more easily than she might in a big open field. Another reason is dog's tiring from lack of stamina when they've been turned a few times; most aren't fit for sustained running.

This is why many lurchers are superior to greyhounds at catching all kinds of creatures as they've usually more stamina and often more brains, despite a slower top speed. The Lurcher learns to run clever from experience, whereas many greyhounds are not allowed free access to areas where they might put up hares or rabbits, denying them the same level of experience. They're kept away from much free running in fields in case they get injured or hurt, yet I believe you need to take that risk. Coursing men don't want their greyhounds to see much action outside regulated meetings as they don't want their dogs to learn to 'run clever'. Running clever, as I put it, means learning to run in such a way that the dog learns the best way to catch whatever quarry he's chasing. Greyhounds are much faster than hares, but without a lot of experience, invariably run straight at the hare. The hare then turns abruptly causing the dog to overshoot the turn by some yards, giving the hare an advantage of whatever time it takes for the dog to get back on terms. With experience, the dog can learn to run alongside the hare and wait until she makes a mistake, before committing himself and thus giving him a much better chance of a catch and less overshooting. This is running clever. In coursing meetings, the dog that is in front when the hare makes his first turn usually wins, so a coursing trainer certainly doesn't want his dog learning to run alongside the hare as it would let the dog behind him make the hare turn first as he was running straight at it.

Dusty, as I said, developed this knack of catching and I don't know how many hares he caught, but it was a lot and the area at the time was teeming with wildlife other than rabbits as myxomatosis had practically obliterated them. Dusty and his brother took a fair number of foxes too.

Dusty wasn't big, about 64 lbs, but was leggy and athletic for his size. He was a predominantly black dog. We ran him mostly at Dunmore over the 435 two bend course that was well suited to strong galloping types as the finish had a slight uphill gradient. Many people travelled to Dunmore thinking they'd have a chance there if their dog didn't get 525 yards, but with that uphill finish, a dog needed to get at least 500. Dunmore is sadly no more and it's a pity as it was ahead of its time as a running surface. It was a big wide all sand galloping track, more typical of something you'd see in Australia. Dusty started slowly as a pup and had a bad experience with the door of the traps hitting him when schooling and as a result, he was always last out of the boxes. I can't remember what times he was doing but he lost his first two races after walking out of the traps and catching the eye by making up a huge amount of ground and was ahead at the pickup in both. He won next time out despite a repeat performance at the traps and won easily. Again, I can't recall the time, but I remember my Da being approached afterwards by a couple of different men looking to buy the dog. Initially, he said no, but succumbed shortly after as he needed the money. Speaking to him years later about this, he said another factor in his decision to sell was the lack of staying races available at the time and he lamented the fact he'd sold the dog far too cheaply. There were plenty of sprint races and 525's, but even 550's were scarce unless it was an open event and it was obvious to him that Dusty was going to need longer distances to fulfil his potential. Sometime later I remember being in the bookies with my Da and watching Dusty win an open stayers race at either Harringay or Hackney (I can't remember which). My Da backed him that day and won a few quid, but always regretted selling the dog.

I also remember, around this time, a small blue brindled bitch called Buffy Marie (named after the Native American folk singer) who won a sprint stake at Dungannon. She was a lively little 54-pound bitch who was by Ceili Band out of a coursing bitch. Lively Band (Ceili Band's sire) had famously fought in a big race and there were some doubts over the progeny of this sire line, but this bitch was very genuine and gutsy. She too was sold soon after.

A lot of people reckon that good rearing can only be done on farms where the dogs have open access to wide spaces, but I can tell you that many champion dogs were reared in and around Belfast in terraced houses and undoubtedly many more in other urban areas in the UK and Ireland. As long as pups get the chance to gallop daily, it matters not where they sleep.

Interestingly, in these times there were no complete dog meals available as there are today. Men fed their race dogs on brown bread and raw beef. There was mixer type biscuit meal such as Winalot, but you had to add meat to it and it wasn't favoured by doggy men of this time. I remember us going to Cobb's Pet store (which is long gone) on the Crumlin Road for the loaves of unsliced brown bread, which was broken up and soaked in hot water or tea, then mixed with the meat and sometimes a raw egg and usually a drop of cod liver oil. Pups would usually get a cheaper, fattier grade of meat or tripe mixed with the bread. It was believed at the time that many badly reared dogs and pups were fed a diet that consisted of just bread and milk.

My Granny lived off Springfield Road in West Belfast, and we lived there too for a time. I remember there was a Peter Pan bakery around the corner and local greyhound men knew it was a source of cheap bread for their dogs (and probably themselves too). A fella was working there and if you went to him and asked for a bag of dog bread, he'd take a black bag and fill it full, not only of brown bread but often soda's, potato bread, pancakes and whatever it took to fill the bag. Dog bread, as it was called, should have been bread that was taken off shop shelves for losing its freshness, or maybe damaged, but this fella would never refuse you! If he had no dog bread, he'd take fresh bread off the conveyor belts, making the odd hole here and there with a stick as if to justify giving it to you. He must have cost the bakery thousands. Maybe that's why it closed down a few years later. A black bag full of this bread cost ten pence in the late seventies.

Things improved on the work front for my Da and he started to make decent money working for himself painting and papering, as they call it in Belfast. He found a small paint company in Liverpool that made decent paint at low prices and started buying it in pallets to use on jobs, and he also started selling it from the house directly to the public via a small ad in the Irish News daily paper. This later led to the opening of a couple of paint and wallpaper shops in the city and the family's fortunes looked a little brighter. The shops did well for a few years before the big sheds and multinationals started to pop up everywhere. They offered plenty of parking and big stores to walk around with no obligation to buy.

Later on, in my teens, the family moved down south to the Irish Republic and opened a shop in Navan in Co. Meath in 1990, in which I was instrumental to its success as for the first couple of years my Da continued to paint houses whilst I sold paint in the shop. The business did well and specialised in decent quality paint and wallpaper at really low prices, which was ahead of its time as there were no B&Q's, Woodie's, or big hardware chains like there are today. They came to the North and the UK a few years ahead of Southern Ireland and Irish prices for most consumer goods at this time were ridiculously high.

Within two years, we opened a second shop in the same town and the business continued to flourish. This enabled my parents to buy a house with four acres of land about three miles outside Kells in Co. Meath. It was at this time that we initially bought two sapling pups and started to build a kennel in earnest with paddocks and utilised outbuildings already there. These worked great as kennels with a stable for a whelping bay. Later on, we had a kennel block constructed that further improved our facility.

The saplings that I refer to above were bought from an advertisement in the Sporting Press. They were five months old by Bold Rabbit x Rhincrew Spark. The 'Rhincrew' prefix belongs to the Barry family outside Youghal in County Cork and they are synonymous with the Skipping Chick dam line that included Lemon Soda and many prolific producers of early pace for many generations. What was remarkable about this dam line was its propensity to produce open class winners from bitches that were moderate or average on the track themselves. The skipping chick line had some coursing blood in it. Another more recent dam line I regard as similar to this one is the Minnie's Nikita dam line that also produced flying machines in many instances from bitches that had no racing ability themselves or who were littermates of an exceptional dog or bitch. Bold Rabbit at the time was a very fast son of Whisper Wishes out of a top-class bitch called 'Contact Breaker' who ran in a top company in England. Bold Rabbit wasn't long at stud at the time, so was unproven as they say. I travelled down to Youghal with a girlfriend and picked out two dog pups, a fawn and a black and gave seven hundred pounds for the pair. Both littermates won races. The fawn dog (Lucky Fawn) won more races, but only got about 350 yards before blowing up. The black dog (Solitary Man) won a good race in Navan over 525 in 29.50 (TR 29.10 at the time) but lacked a couple of yards of early to the first bend to avoid a lot of the trouble he found in races. He was the faster of the two though, if not just as tough and determined.

The Barry family offered me a brood bitch to lease (Rhincrew Exile) who was by Knockrour Slave out of a daughter of Skipping Chick. The terms were a dog pup back at twelve weeks. We decided to mate her to 'Make History' who had won the 1988 Irish Derby over 550 and previously won the Puppy Derby over 525 yards. Despite his quality, his first crop of runners was considered by breeders to be a tad disappointing, but my Da reckoned this was partly due to the fact he was based in Armagh in Northern Ireland, which limited his appeal as very few Irish breeders will travel north as has always been the case since the likes of the brilliant Newdown Heather. Likewise, the great I'm Slippy started his stud career in Northern

Ireland but was wisely moved to Cork, where he became one of Ireland's best sires, particularly of early pace.

Our litter only yielded two pups, a dark brindled dog and an almost pure white bitch named Sneachta Ban (Snow White in Irish). The bitch was very decent and won about 50% of her early races which included a 29.70 at Harolds cross at sixteen months, which was a good run on the old grass track in winter. She was third in a very good, graded bitch stake at Shelbourne Park that was won by a bitch called 'Fusion' who later became a terrific bitch winning many open races. Fusion was from the same litter as Ratify who was the best-staying dog in Ireland of his genre and broke four track records as well as winning many top races including the Cesarewitch 600 in Navan (twice). He was also a decent stud dog from limited opportunities. Limited because Irish breeders were loath to using stayers.

It's difficult to know how good Sneachta Ban would have become as she got a bad injury after only a handful of races and she'd shown improvement in every win. The bitch Fusion wasn't very much ahead of her and she turned out to be one of the top bitches in

Ireland. Sneachta won in Shelbourne Park, Navan and Harolds Cross. We entered her in a coursing oaks bitch trial stake in Cavan and she made the semi-finals. She was then taken to Mullingar for a 550 yards race and was three lengths in front going into the first bend but went unsighted between the first and second bends and was knocked over the hare rail by a dog running into her when she slowed down looking for the bunny. There was a lot of money for another dog in the race and I've no doubts that her 'accident' was the work of the hare driver speeding up the hare, as it approached the first bend enough to make her lose sight of it as she reached the turn. But, how do you prove these things? I gave the hare driver a bollocking; but what was the point? She was badly injured in this race with a torn muscle and was never the same again. Her litter brother wasn't in the same class. He had no early pace but was above average for a pup over 525 and really motored down the back straight. He was sold to England where he would get longer graded races.

We never got the chance to breed Sneachta Ban as she was later savaged in a kennel fight and had to be put down. I always lamented this fact as I think she'd have made a great brood. She was about 59 lbs and a really good-looking bitch with a great temperament and a genuine attitude. She had that rare commodity in greyhounds with good early pace and staying ability. I remember having her over the fields when she was about eight months old and she got a chase at a rabbit and I couldn't find her. I searched the fields around for ages, but in the end, had to head home. When I got there, she was in the feed kitchen with her head stuck in a bag of milk powder!

As there were only two pups in the litter, (all leasing agreements stipulate there must be at least four pups to a litter to give a pup to the owner of the brood bitch) the Barry family didn't get a pup this time. Instead, it was agreed we would hang onto the bitch and breed her again next time she came in season and hopefully get a bigger litter. We mated her again to a son of Yellow Band named Moneypoint Coal, but there were no resulting pups and we gave her back along with a pup from another litter we bred ourselves from another bitch to ensure the family got something back. This bitch 'Rhincrew Exile' was probably the easiest going greyhound I've ever seen, who would (unusually for a greyhound) just follow you around the yard, sit outside and never wander off. The Barry family would later come to prominence again from the 'Skipping Chick' days with Rhincrew Sean who won a very good Produce Stakes in Clonmel and other open races. They were nice people from a farming background and when I went down that day and bought the pups, as was typical of so many greyhound folks, they fed us a huge feed when the deal was done. This I remember well because we'd stopped on route to break the journey and had eaten shortly before we arrived at the Barry home; we were stuffed! The table was laid and to refuse would have caused offence, so another feed was had.

In the early '90s, the Sporting Press newspaper was the only dedicated greyhound weekly paper. As the spreadsheet of the Irish Coursing Club (ICC) it was very conservative and old fashioned, rubbish really, but we had nothing else in which to buy and sell greyhounds. It's still going today and no better in my opinion. There was the UK monthly Greyhound Star that was a magazine with plenty of colour and it was much better all-round, but of no use for buying or selling stock in Ireland. The only other paper that proved useful for advertising racing dogs, was the UK daily 'Sporting Life' which had a small greyhound supplement. It was good if you wanted to sell a young racer that had just won a night or two beforehand. The Sporting Life was later replaced by the Racing Post and it's still going today.

We saw advertised a stud dog called 'North Line' who was a son of Sandman out of Cooga Customer. He was a 1984, black and white dog who had finished second in the 1986 Produce Stakes Final and had won an Open event in HX in 29.04 (grass), which was near the track record at the time. He was a top-class dog who had been sold for ten thousand pounds as a pup in 1986. He had an even better litter brother, a dog called Lodge Prince who smashed the TR at Wimbledon in the English Derby in 28.34 for 525 and also the 550 clock at Shelbourne in 30.03. Both these records stood for many years, which shows how freakishly fast of a dog he was. Ultimately, in 1990, Lodge Prince was considered a failure at stud as he'd covered plenty of bitches and didn't deliver anything of the calibre of himself, at least not in his early crop. He later sired Farloe Melody who won the English Derby and went to Australia to stand at stud, but overall despite some good offspring was disappointing at stud. This we knew but reckoned his brother North Line would be a good addition to our future breeding plans. Rightly or wrongly, we always believed that the same blood gave you the same chance. Many litter sisters of top-class dogs produce top dogs, so we reckoned that North Line could produce (potentially anyway) as well as his more illustrious brother.

We bought North Line, who was six at the time for a grand. He was a lovely big dog with a super temperament. We travelled down to Thurles in Tipperary to get him and this was our first introduction to Donal Cummins. Donal was a character and always looking for a way to make easy money. A small man and a fast talker, I particularly remember his distinctive and abundant black hair sprouting out of each nostril, and there were dogs everywhere you looked. He had an almost brand new expensive jeep that was destroyed inside from dogs and a horrible smell to which he seemed oblivious!

There was a shed there with two young litters and their mothers in opposite corners, totally open. I remember asking him if he wasn't concerned in case one of the pups strayed over to the wrong mother. "It'll only happen once," he said. This attitude was and is still typical of many greyhound men in Ireland, who tend to think of greyhounds as a survival of the fittest. Many breeders would let a bitch find her own whelping place, irrespective of suitability. I remember being in one such kennel and the breeder didn't even know one of his bitches had whelped! We found her and pups in the back seat of an old car in one of his fields. They were fine and thriving, but had it been winter it might have been a different story. Such attitudes are pure ignorance and still practised today by many breeders, yet how many pups die from negligence that could easily be saved with a little care and attention?

Donal Cummins tried to sell us everything he had. My ears pricked up when he showed us a brindled bitch called Greenpark Betty, who was a litter sister to Greenpark Fox who had been the best sprinter in Ireland for many years, but more importantly was making huge waves on the stud scene and was siring fast dogs over all distances, which belied the common view that sprinters only produced short distance runners.

Betty was heading for four years of age and had raced in minor open class (and won) in England herself, but had never had a litter. My Da knew very little about bloodlines. All he was interested in was whether a dog could run or not, although he liked the idea of us breeding our own dogs. I used to spend hours reading any greyhound publications I could and trying to analyse the different bloodlines.

Everyone in greyhounds today is familiar with and uses the Greyhound Data website, which is brilliant for researching any bloodline. In the early 1990s, there was no internet for the masses and everyone's knowledge of a pedigree would have been limited to usually two generations, excepting the very rare occasions when a breeder would have his own dam line going back generations. Today people can analyse pedigrees as far back as they want and find out the results of littermates, see racing videos and access all manner of statistics through this single website. It certainly enables breeders to be better informed, but does it make it any easier to breed good greyhounds? I know plenty that would say statistics don't win races.

I told my Da we had to have that bitch and she changed hands for six hundred. If I could have seen the future that day I would have left her there, but more about that later. We gave him eighteen hundred that day and also obtained a six-month-old sapling dog pup by Balalika who was at stud there. Balalika had broken the track record at Clonmel over 525 in 28.68 and had been a hot favourite to win a couple of major competitions but seemed unlucky in finals. He was an early paced son of Moral Support, a remarkable sire who had probably the best strike rate of any, on a pup per pup ratio, but was a poor server and would refuse many of the bitches that came to him. He was always in the top twenty sire listings from very few runners, which is the true test of a good sire. Balalika, his son had a good initial start to his stud career with some very fast pups and his stud fee rocketed to seven hundred and fifty pounds, which was amongst the highest in the country. Sadly, for him, few of the early crop won major competitions and the dog fell out of favour with breeders and his stud fee went down again. Some of his pups were on the small side, but despite some very good smaller dogs, greyhound people like to see big dogs. It's a bit like a farmer buying a calf; he'll never buy the smallest one. We had mostly very good luck with the Balalika sired pups we had, as you'll hear in the pages to come. The fawn and white pup we bought was a 1990 whelp out of a bitch called Glebe girl and we named him Steve's Champ (I had a younger brother called Steve). Strangely, his pedigree or this litter to his dam doesn't show on Greyhound Data, but we ended up selling him for two and a half thousand pounds when he won a 600 at Mullingar in 33.92 (grass), which was a very good run as at the time 34 secs was rarely broken (TR 33.61). We would later break this track record with a different dog, but more about that in a while. Champ was a nervous dog and didn't like strangers, which is a rarity in greyhounds although nervousness does show up sometimes. He was only back in our kennels a couple of days and we let him loose with some other pups, thinking by this stage it was safe to do so. We couldn't get him to come back to us. He would come to within about five feet and stay there. If we took a step towards him, back he would go and come to within five feet of us, again and again. Not sure which of us came up with the idea, but eventually my youngest brother who was about five at the time was put in the field with a lead. As is often the case with nervous dogs, he went straight to the child and allowed him to lead him. Dogs almost always seem to know that children are no threat to them and I've never come across a greyhound that wasn't reliable with children, despite breed books stating the contrary. There's a common ignorance with people who don't have experience with greyhounds to assume that because they wear muzzles when racing that they're somehow vicious or unreliable with people, rather than the real reason being that when the hare stops and goes into the escape, dogs will often fight with each other when unsighted.

Champ was a small dog, about sixty-four pounds weight (29 KG) and although some details are sketchy in my mind, I remember he showed remarkable improvement in schooling. A lot of pups will improve a second at best from initial schooling to starting racing, but he improved a second and a half before his first race. To the horse racing fraternity, such time means nothing, nor does it mean anything to anyone outside of greyhound racing, but as anyone involved in it knows, half a second is the difference between a good dog and a great one. Anyway, Champ won six from ten races, culminating with the 33.92, 600 win at Mullingar. Gerry Leech, the control steward at Mullingar track at the time bought the dog for English connections. Strangely, I saw he was down to run in another 600 at Mullingar the following week and rang the track to say he was sold and gone to England. I was told he was back (I never found out the mechanics of what happened) and was now being trained by local trainer Francie Murray. But he never topped what he'd done for us and I feel the dog must have got injured shortly afterwards as he seemed to disappear from the scene. I don't think he won another race come to think of it. Within a couple of months, I saw another interesting advertisement in the Sporting Press. I remember the rather understated ad as if it was yesterday.

Brood bitch for sale. Game Ball x Raymond's Pride. Bitch proven.

I realised from the breeding that this bitch was a litter sister to Make History, the already mentioned 1988 Derby winner. I immediately phoned the Kilkenny number and did a deal over the phone, agreeing to buy the bitch for five hundred and fifty pounds. She was being sold by her breeder Raymond Dowling, an elderly man who told me the dam Raymond's Pride had won many top races at Shelbourne Park over 575 yards and had produced open class in every litter. He had a half-sister for sale too by Brilliant Chimes X Raymond's Pride and tried to sell me her as well, but I didn't bite. Raymond's Pride had another son at stud, Love-a-Sailor by Shamrock Sailor.

Interestingly, the bitch I bought (Racefield Kate) had a litter of pups also for sale by Kyle Jack and he tried to sell me some of these too. One of these pups (Centreback) later won the Midland Puppy Derby in Mullingar over 550 and ran second to the great Lisglass Lass in the Irish Laurels final at Cork. I could have bought him that day for three hundred and fifty pounds!

Centreback was probably the fastest dog that Kate produced, although the rest of the litter all won races, there was nothing else in the litter close to Centreback's ability (his sire 'Kyle Jack' was a good winner of the Irish Derby and proved to be a decent sire for all distances with early pace). He was only sixty-three pounds in weight and suffered from track leg, but he had superb early and back straight pace. A **'track leg'** is a soft tissue swelling on the inside of the tibia caused when the outside of the elbow hits the inside of the back leg when galloping or racing. He would always run with a smear of Vaseline on the afflicted area that enabled the limbs to slide off each other. As far as I'm aware, none of Racefield Kate's other pups had this condition.

Racefield Kate had the first litter to Carters Lad and these all won races but were pretty ordinary and her owner probably thought she wasn't going to produce top class, hence the decision to sell her. She was nothing much to look at, compared with her derby winning brother who looked like a champion should look. She had no race form either apart from a couple of trials on her card. He told me she had problem toes and was always breaking down, but she been decent enough (they always tell you that, rightly or wrongly!). Her feet were poor looking, but as far as I was concerned the same blood flowed through her as what produced her double classic winning brother. She was about sixty pounds in weight and quite low to the ground, not leggy like her brother.

Not long after this, I spotted another ad that seemed too tempting to pass up. Two five-month-old bitch saplings by Balalika x Ese Whisper. Ese Whisper had been a finalist in the English Oaks and her brother had run well in the English Derby. The two bitches were on the small side but looked keen and we duly picked them up. The couple we bought the pups from needed a lot of paint for their house as it turned out, which we supplied, so this cut their price by a couple of hundred. The two bitches weighed fifty-one pounds and fifty-four pounds, pretty small for racing, where fifty-eight to sixty is about the average racing weight for bitches.

The smaller of the two was a black & white bitch and was the fastest, but she had a kink or a fault to her that made sure she never realised her potential. She was quite nervy and highly strung and if she got the slightest bump, she seemed to go to pieces and wouldn't go past another dog. She was fine if she got out in front, but the minute another dog got close to her, it unsettled her and her chance was gone. I've mixed feelings about why this was. On one hand, I feel if she was genuinely chasing hard, she wouldn't have been expecting a thump or bump and it wouldn't have been a problem, but the other dogs in the kennel would bully her if they got the chance, so she was soft, to say the least. She could run though and had serious early pace. We entered her in a 325-yard twelve dog sprint sweepstake at Mullingar, where there were two heats and the first three from each heat made up the final six. She won her heat in nineteen seconds, which was decent for a debut race, but she was capable of about 18.70, which was open class. In the final, she didn't break well and never showed due to her quirkiness. She went to England shortly after to a graded kennel, where they run every week for appearance money. I can't remember what we got for her, but it was probably a bit more than what she cost us.

Her sister Whispering Grass, as she was named, was a fawn bitch and was a real good looker for her fifty-four pounds weight. She was racy, game-looking and turned out a decent bitch. She won first time out at Mullingar over 325 and won again the same week in 29.60 over 525 in Navan by a distance! (It was obviously a very poor pup's race) and she was only fifteen months old. She won a good few races, but only stayed about 470 yards fully. She developed great early pace and overcame poor trapping in her early races. She was an inside runner, who if housed anywhere other than trap, one would immediately move inwards to the left and rail so tight she almost touched the rails. As there was no seeding in Ireland at this time, this was a big disadvantage and she did find trouble at times in races that she could've easily won. She did though win close to 50% of her races, so genuine was she in her desire to win. Her best win was a 29.90 at Mullingar in a decent Saturday night race, where she overcame a trap six draw and blasted out of the traps so quickly she got across to the inside rail without colliding with any of the other dogs. 29.90 for 525 might sound slow today, but Mullingar at this time was grass and it was the slowest surface in Ireland and had the tightest bends in the country. It suited a certain type of dog, usually not too big. If you could break thirty seconds over 525 at Mullingar you had a decent dog. To put it in perspective as far as class goes, the top open events over 525 at Mullingar at this time would rarely be won in better than 29.50 and these would be the top dogs in the country. Whispering Grass was just a couple of lengths off being in this company but was a joy to train and take racing as she was rarely without a chance. She developed a wrist injury that curtailed her a bit after her first dozen or so races and coming in season twice a year didn't help her accumulate that many starts. I leased her out to an acquaintance that frequented Navan track as he had won a service in a raffle to a dog called Glencorbry Celt. He was a rangy black son of Brilliant Chimes that finished runner up in one of the last Irish Derbies ran over 525 yards, before they changed it to 550 and was a well-proven sire of decent progeny, if not spectacular. He was handled at stud by his trainer Jerry Melia, who seemed a nice man along with being very knowledgeable. He told us that the dog suffered from something in his chest, similar to asthma, that the dog always ran better when the going was soft and the weather wet. His superb 29.08 Derby semi-final win was by far the fastest on the rain-sodden grass of Shelbourne Park (1984). Interestingly, he only ever sired blue or black offspring, so strong was his genetic colour imprinting. I travelled with the bitch and saw the mating, but unfortunately, she didn't conceive. We tried mating her sometime later to Strange Dilly, but she missed again and we didn't try to breed her again. With hindsight, I regret not persevering a bit harder to get her in pup, but I had plenty on my plate at this time and there was also the possibility she might have thrown small pups, not being the biggest herself.

The period between 1990 and 1994 was largely a magical time for us and our kennel. To begin with, our burgeoning paint business partly subsidised our initial outlay and purchasing of pups and brood bitches. Once we had our few acres and kennel facilities, it made a huge difference to us being able to prioritise our time. In 1990, I was eighteen. We had two retail outlets that had to be staffed and stocked six days a week, as well as a small greyhound kennel. Usually, we'd spend two hours working the dogs in the morning and another two in the afternoon or early evening. The shop work and greyhound work were divided equally between us. My brother Steven who was eight years my junior helped out a bit as well with feeding and paddocking.

The success we had from our investment if you want to call it that, was amazing. We didn't win any classics, but all of the pups we bought and most of the early home-breeds won first time out. At one time our winning percentage of pups winning their first race was around 70%, which if you're experienced in greyhounds, you know seldom happens. It was vital that we got some degree of early success or there would have been a lot fewer dogs bought. Any money we won or got from selling dogs was refunnelled into the operation. We were gearing up to be in a position where we would have pups coming thick and fast in the next couple of years, and winning and selling on was necessary as we didn't have the time to concentrate on very many race dogs.

What did we do to win so many races?

Our pups were very fit from an early age. From they were inoculated and had their ears marked, we had them out in the fields every day, often twice a day and they could do what they wanted. They could run themselves ragged or do nothing at all. Usually, they engaged in chasing games that were permitted as long as there was no bullying, which happens often enough. The smallest in the litter will often end up hunted by the others if they're allowed to do it. So, our dogs were paddock reared in a reasonably sized paddock of 150 feet in length by approx. 50 feet wide. This gave some scope for exercise in itself, but the free-running once or twice a day out of the paddocks I think makes a big difference to rearing pups as they get complacent in the same surroundings and get bored even in the biggest field if that's all they ever see. Greyhounds are essentially sprinters and run in short bursts. Letting the dogs out once or twice a day like this ensured they used themselves in these times.

Many Irish greyhound people want their dogs reared with 'full freedom' as they call it, where the dogs are reared almost as if wild over a large acreage. Sometimes this rearing results in the pups rarely seeing or having any contact with people, and whilst I'm in favour of pups getting the opportunity to run and hunt as much as they want, this lack of human contact is not a good thing. Pups need handling. I've seen many nervous and useless dogs come out of this system due to the dogs being too wild or almost feral to ever adapt to racing as the handling of them comes too late for them to accept it and they never become comfortable with it. Other rearing in Ireland consists of pups never getting out of the confines of their paddocks, due to either laziness of the rearer or a lack of time due to looking after too many dogs. This happens a lot more often than people realise.

When they got to about 9-10 months, we'd put them up the field after the drag lure and they'd get well galloped for 2-3 weeks before going to the track for their first-hand slip, followed by schooling. In schooling pups we'd start with sprints, 325 or 350 yards, working up to 525, when we felt they were ready. We gave three schooling trials a fortnight, which some people think is too much, but we very rarely got an injury, and I think if our pups weren't so fit when commencing these trials, we would have gotten more injuries. The only deviation in this would be if we had a very big pup, we might not start him for a month or two later, at thirteen or fourteen months and stick to one trial per week if we thought it best. Obviously, if we thought a pup was looking a bit jaded or sore, it would be rested.

We had a double set of starting traps at home and we had them in the middle of the field (fixed open) that led from the paddocks to the field we used for galloping, so the pups got used to running in and out through them from an early age. When schooling time came, they weren't too bothered about them and usually adapted to them pretty quickly, with the odd exception.

Once we were happy a pup was genuinely chasing properly, we'd give it a trial hand slip just in front of the traps and clock the run and see how far off qualifying it was, or in some cases if we had something special. On a couple of occasions, we qualified pups first time out of a box if they clocked well inside qualifying in their hand slip, but usually, they'd need a bit of experience coming out of the traps in order to qualify. Most pups will lose half a second trapping in the early days. Our goal was always to get them qualifying as early as possible in order to capitalise on as much improvement as possible in the six weeks from qualifying before their first race. Two qualifying trials would be the norm, one over a sprint of 325 or 350 yards, followed by a 525.

We very rarely stopped pups in qualifying trials and if we did, it was by natural methods of feeding. Milk and sugar provided about an hour and a half before a run would slow down any dog. Care is needed with this concoction as too much will make the dog cramp and also take away too much time. We never used tablets or pills to slow a dog down, except one time, which I'll get to later on.

For the first few times in the boxes, one of us would always stand to the side in front, so the dog could see us and this greatly negated the possibility of the dog turning around and facing the wrong way when the traps opened, or if the dog (as often happens in early days) had already turned in the time it took us to load the dog in the box and come to the front of him, we'd call him and quickly flick his tail (through the trap bars) to get him to turn around again. Once the dog can see the handler, he usually won't turn back around, but some can do it from being hyper when hearing the bunny approaching.

One thing that I must address here that other greyhound books written by more famous trainers don't; no trainer can turn a bad dog into a good one and we were lucky that when we put our kennel together, we started off with mostly decent pups. Try sending Jose Mourinho to manage a team in the lower tiers of English or Scottish football with no money and see how well he does! It's the same thing and relative to greyhounds.

There are dogs bred that are chasing mad, but simply too slow to qualify and no one can change that. I believe that pups are born with whatever ability they're destined to have and good rearing and management will capitalise on this and draw out this ability over time.

We lived quite close to both Mullingar (about 15 miles) and Navan (13 miles) and these were our main haunts. Longford was about an hour away and we'd sometimes trial and occasionally race there just for a change of scenery for the dogs. We were also about an hour and a quarter from the Dublin tracks and would sometimes use them too, but never for a debut race as it was always harder to win there and it took longer to get there for trials.

We were consistent with what we did. The dogs were fed and exercised at the same time every day. They were well handled as pups and got plenty of attention. They were well contented. This last point is often overlooked, but dogs need to feel secure in their surroundings and many of the dogs we bred ourselves didn't take well to the English racing routine (when sold on), where they're handled less and spend much more time in kennels. A few times, dogs came back to us after an unsuccessful spell in England and usually won races with us afterwards. It was purely a case of them being unable to settle.

We only fed race dogs once per day. If a dog was racing that night, he'd get an egg in the morning with some glucose mixed in and get the main meal later that night after racing.

At this time, we fed Purina brand of dog meal, which was a good quality feed and the dogs did well on it with thick, glossy coats which is always an indication something is working. Once a pup had qualified, his feed would also be supplemented by raw beef that was supplied by the local kennels of the Meath hunt that was only a couple of miles away. This meat, known as knacker meat (the original term comes from dead horses) was usually from cows, minced and put into ten-pound bags. Recently, I read the book about Nick Savva by Floyd Amphlett, and he states that he wouldn't use it as he only uses that fit for human consumption, but I don't know any trainer or breeder in Ireland that doesn't use it. We certainly never had any problems with it, nor had the money or the morals to refuse it. To only feed meat fit for human consumption is akin to wiping your arse with five-pound notes.

Once a pup qualified, she'd be washed for fleas, freshly wormed and given the daily meat supplement of about a pound's worth. Raw meat does make dogs a bit more aggressive and will aid in dropping a dog's weight if need be with a reduction in meal and increase in meat. We always liked a pup to carry a pound or two excess weight into a qualifying trial, but no more than that. This weight would be shed before the pup would race. The pup would also be vomited with a lump of baking soda (to get rid of the build-up of bile) about a week before the race. There are mixed opinions to this practice, but I've often seen a couple of lengths of improvement by doing it. Other times there's no improvement.

Once the pup qualified, the trialling would be stepped up to three trials a fortnight and concentrated on whichever track we'd decided to race the pup at.

The tracks

We would alternate racing between Navan and Mullingar; one being sand and one grass gave the pups the experience of both surfaces. As already stated, sometimes we'd go to Longford for trials on Sunday mornings but didn't really like it as there was always a long wait to get onto the track. Longford has always been a very good running and well-maintained track that continues to this day. If the distance and waiting times were less, we'd have used it a lot more as it was a very safe track for pups to learn on, whereas Mullingar with its tight turns, particularly so on the third bend (later to be realigned) wasn't the best and many dogs got injured in Mullingar. We were pretty lucky regarding injuries and only Sneachta Ban got badly hurt there. Private trials at Longford at this time were conducted on a Sunday morning and the queues there most Sunday mornings were off-putting, to say the least.

Navan was an all sand track and a very good galloping type circuit. It was, however, operated on a shoestring with minimal investment or money spent on its infrastructure by its syndicate of owners. They even sold their alcohol licence at one point and from that time on could only sell soft and hot drinks, which is laughable really when you think about it. It was a spartan place with little comfort. It was well known here that if you had a pup that did a fast run on a Saturday morning, he'd be a short price come race night and often your chance to bet on your own dog was snatched before your very eyes by someone who knew as much about your dog as you did! A few times at Navan I made a move towards the bookies only for someone to jump in ahead of me and the dog would be wiped off the board. Many of the bookies at the smaller provincial tracks would only take a maximum of a hundred quid (some would only take fifty) and wouldn't lay any more. There were many unscrupulous characters at Navan who only went there looking to cash in on someone else's hard work and ultimate misfortune. The owners eventually cashed in and the track was sold to developers in 1999 but lay untouched for many years until Lidl bought it and opened there in 2010. Why the track wasn't leased back and continue to operate in those intervening years is a mystery to me.

By contrast, Mullingar was in a better geographical area as it's roughly the centre of Ireland and drew patrons and dogs from a much bigger catchment area than did Navan, although Navan was a better track as far as running surfaces went. Mullingar always was better managed and obtained much better sponsors. Their tea room and bar were much busier than the Navan one ever was and they'd have music on Saturday nights that lasted well after the last race was run. Mullingar track had an atmosphere, Navan had none.

We tended to avoid the Dublin tracks of Harolds Cross and Shelbourne Park as it was not only harder to win there, but it took an hour and a half each way to get there amid plenty of traffic. We did take some of our better race dogs with experience, but never a pup for a first race as Navan and Mullingar were so much easier for us to get to and our pups were thoroughly schooled there that they would come to know the track where they would race at very well beforehand.

A tale of two brood bitches

During the period, 1990 to 1994 our breeding endeavours mainly involved the two brood bitches we'd purchased specifically to that end.

Greenpark Betty

She was a 1986 daughter of Citizen Supreme and Stern Satoo (who turned out a decent producer despite being a moderate performer herself). Betty raced in top grade and minor open class in England and was a litter sister to Greenpark Fox who had been the best early paced dog in Ireland for many years and had broken four sprint track records. There were other open class performers in the litter also up to 550 yards. As a sire, Greenpark Fox was a success and produced several very fast offspring for all distances. His greatest son was probably 'Manx Treasure' who won a very good Irish Derby over 550 yards carrying an injury. There were people, however, who didn't like the dog as a sire and I noticed Nick Savva in his book stated he regarded this sire line (Bright Lad) as somewhat ingenuine. This was news to me, as I never really heard any criticism of Greenpark Fox as a stud dog during his time at stud. It does though make perfect sense to me now as you're about to read.

As I already said, we purchased Betty at the same time as the stud dog 'North Line', buying both from Donal Cummins in Thurles Co. Tipperary. It only seemed right and natural to mate the two as they were not closely related. North Line was a son of the hugely successful American import 'Sandman'. Sandman had been possibly the best sire Ireland had ever had up to this point (definitely the best imported one), so influential was his producing potency. An interesting aside about Sandman is he was from a superb litter and he was a sprinter by American standards, running over 550 yards, which he barely got. American's tend to breed for 660 yards and Sandman was a third or fourth string in his litter as far as ability goes. He would have had no value or patronage in America as a stud dog and that's why he ended up in Ireland. Most early imports to Ireland of American or Australian stud dogs were of poor quality in racing ability. He was a small dog too, only about

64 lbs. These facts, of course, are immaterial as he was a revelation at stud, but just goes to show that there are many exceptions to what greyhound people regard as being important or necessary. Size doesn't always matter in greyhounds.

The North Line x Greenpark Betty litter were whelped in June 1991 and there were seven pups in the litter. The colours were black, white & black, brindle and white and brindle. There was only one bitch in the litter. I remember they were a very even litter of decent size, the dogs ranged from 68 (smallest) to 75 lbs and the bitch was about 60. They were robust, strong pups with great temperaments and were very easily reared. They loved to run and had a fantastic rearing full of galloping and free of injury or sickness. They were introduced to the drag lure at about nine months of age and all took to it like mad, which gave us a great heart for their future. They had also hunted rabbits in the fields around us with equal desire and had pulled down a fox between them at eight months.

Unfortunately, our initial enthusiasm was short-lived. Only one of the pups chased when taken to the track for the first time, despite their keenness on the drag. The rest of them wouldn't look at it, absolutely no interest in it whizzing past them whatsoever! We tried everything, from getting them more hunting experience in the fields to numerous experiments on private schooling tracks. We even had the electric hare pass them at walking speed (which will often lead to an increase in keenness) and still, they showed no interest. The one dog (racing name Steve's North) who did initially chase wasn't genuine and sometimes chased and sometimes didn't depending on his mood. What made this all the harder and more disconcerting was the fact that they could all run and had huge pace. We knew this as they could easily beat older race dogs with ability up the field after the drag. We also coursed them at coursing meetings, despite them being very young. One of them reached the last 8 of a 32 dog Derby Trial stake at Trim at 14 months and was narrowly beaten by the eventual winner. Another one was beaten at the Dundalk Derby Trial Stake by a short head. These outings were against older, experienced, coursing bred pups. Our litter had no problems chasing the live hare!

Only Steve's North made it as a race dog. He won a 525 in around 30 secs (average for a pup's race) and only chased from the third bend home but came from way off the pace to win. We entered him in a dual distance stake at Mullingar over 525 and 550. He finished second in his 525 and came with a huge finish in the 550 final to finish third, about a length of the winner. In both these races, he was in front of the pick-up.

When you have a pup like this, it's very easy to be fooled into thinking he just needs staying races and has no early pace, but we knew differently! His next race was a 600 at Mullingar on a Saturday night and again he only put the head down fully halfway down the back straight and made up his six lengths deficit in a matter of strides and won going away by six at the finish in 34.02, which was decent and a very good run for a youngster. If you were breaking 34 secs over 600 at this time, you had a decent dog. When you consider, he was only trying after the halfway point, what could he do if trying all the way?

He seemed to stay forever, always scarcely taxed after his races, but then he was only running less than half the distance at top speed. Thing is with dodgy dogs, you never know what you've got with them because there are just too many variables. Was he running flat out at the finish or have more in the tank? Did he just do enough to win? Why do they decide to sometimes chase partway through a race and then plod along behind the field in others? Will he try harder against faster dogs? All of these things go through your head and more.

I saw an open 700-yard stake advertised in Waterford for twelve dogs and I entered him for it. He was about eighteen months at the time. I wanted to see how he would do against decent staying type dogs, thinking he might try harder against better dogs and this perhaps would focus him. As I said, you'll try everything with a dog to make him genuine, but very few dodgy dogs can be fixed and you can never fully trust them. Occasionally, you'll get a pup that needs a bit of convincing, but if they don't overcome this early on they never can be fully trusted as non-chasing becomes a habit as does chasing.

Anyway, he was entered into this 700-yard stake and accepted. I made the three-and-a-half-hour journey, weighed the dog in and went into the bar area to get a cup of tea and a sandwich. Whilst there, I got talking to a track regular and he asked had I a runner, etc. I could see him getting slightly excited when he realised the distance I was after travelling. "You must have a good chance?" he said. I told him the truth about the dog, but he didn't want to believe it. "You'd hardly come down this far now if you didn't feel you had a chance?" he said in as much of a question as a statement. I realised that his mind was made up and it wouldn't matter what I said from this point on, but when he said he'd have a few pounds on him I reminded him of the dog's unpredictability. He had a gleam in his eyes and wouldn't listen.

The race was about halfway down the card, scheduled for about nine in the evening, roughly ninety minutes after kennelling was completed. I went down when it was time and got the dog who looked like he'd been sleeping and got him ready. I always used my own vests and muzzles and had these with me. I went through the motions, walking the dog around until the steward signalled time, checked the dog's earmarks and went to the traps. I glanced up into the bar, which was directly below the traps and got a hearty wave and a smile from my new best friend. I loaded the dog into the traps and could hear the hum of the hare approach. The traps sprang to life, the dog came out last and last he stayed, limply following the field all the way to the escape. I rather meekly collected the dog (and his card) and went straight to the car park and hit the road as soon as I could. He certainly didn't need a bloody drink as much as I did! It was a long road home that night, I can tell you. I stopped at a phone box some way up the road as there were no mobile phones then and let my Da know the score. It was a short conversation.

This was the last straw as far as we were concerned. We'd given the dog a superb rearing and every chance to become genuine but to no avail. He was entered in the sales trials at Shelbourne park over 600 yards. He won his trial in a fairish time on a rain-sodden, very slow track, coming from a good bit behind the field. Once again, he flattered to deceive and always looked good coming from well of the pace to win. I think he made five hundred quid that day on the bench and off he went, never to be heard of again by us.

It was never obvious in his races that this dog wasn't chasing. He wasn't the 'look all around me' type that you often see. We knew from his times when trialling or racing, sometimes he chased, sometimes he didn't. When he did, it was always partial and only for part of the race, always on the run home. What a shame though and a disappointment this litter was as they all had serious pace. The rest of the litter were given away to rabbit hunters and lurcher breeders, where I'm sure they excelled.

You might think that after such a disappointment, we wouldn't breed from Greenpark Betty again, but at whose door should we have laid the blame? This was her first litter and as far as we were concerned, we couldn't be sure she was to blame, or could it be North Line, the sire's fault. Maybe it was just a disastrous mix of blood, the likes of which never to be seen again.

We decided to breed her one more time and again visited Donal Cummins in Thurles to use his stud dog Balalika (by Moral Support x Bondvella). We knew enough at this stage to know when the bitch was ready for mating and I drove straight down one evening and saw the coupling. Cummins offered to board the bitch for a couple of days and mate her again, but I didn't want to do that on two fronts; 1. Having to come back again, 2. I never liked leaving bitches in someone else's care in case something would happen to her. This is standard practice in Ireland and I would board bitches for people myself a bit later on, but I was never happy with it (although I later left bitches myself out of necessity on a couple of occasions). He also suggested I make him a 'Paint agent' that meant I stock him with a range of paint on tick, excepting that which he could manage to sell, at no risk to himself. Needless to say, I declined his proposal and gave him three hundred for the service.

She duly became impregnated and delivered a healthy litter of seven pups, again with only one bitch in the litter. These pups as they grew, quickly thrived and were even better lookers than the previous litter. They were even bigger than the 'North Line' litter and leggier. We advertised the pups at 12 weeks old, which is customary in Ireland as it's usually this time before the pups are fully vaccinated and have had their ears marked.

You rarely see pups advertised younger than twelve weeks old.

This time around, somewhat bitten by the disappointment of the last litter, we were determined not to hold onto too many of them and sold four of the dog pups for £350 each. One of the dog pups we were rearing for someone met an untimely and tragic end. He was galloping in the field and somehow impaled himself on a metal rod that was sticking up out of the ground and died within seconds. It went right through his chest. He was the only black dog and was the smallest of them, not diminutive in any sense, just more finely put together.

There was a lovely dark brindled pup, bought by a Tiler from Strabane, Hugh Casey, who later did some tiling work for us a month or so later. He'd also agreed to buy a bitch sapling we bred from Racefield Kate who'd had a litter to Strange Dilly three months beforehand. When he came to collect the bitch, he refused her as she had a big toe on one of her back feet. I don't know if she was born this way or it happened during rearing, but I do know she was never hurt or lame at any time. The toe looked a bit fatter than the rest, so I guess he assumed she'd hurt it some way, but we don't remember if she did. It certainly made no difference to her later on at schooling age as she had simply stunning early speed had the most ability in her litter, but more about her in the Racefield Kate chapter. The brindled dog pup he bought out of Greenpark Betty probably didn't chase as we never heard anything about him and he didn't win a race.

We kept two pups for ourselves from the litter, a lovely fawn dog we named Big Brutus and an equally nice black and white beautiful leggy bitch we called Betty Buttons. It became apparent that the dog had exceptional speed as he could make up tremendous ground in the fields during hand slips and beat many older dogs up the gallop. This was long before he was old enough to be taken near the track and commence schooling. He was a big dog and raced around seventy-seven pounds. We used to laugh at how greedy he was and would eat everything if allowed to do so. This, however, was taken to extremes, when he was schooling at Navan track in his early education. Navan track had some gipsy caravans semi-permanently stationed behind the start of the back straight near the hare escape. Obviously, there was a fence partitioning the gipsies from the track, but like the rest of the track, it was probably in a state of disrepair and could be easily breached.

Anyway, the trial over, we went to collect the dog by the hare escape and noticed him eating what appeared to be a large human turd. He was licking his lips and the smell from it was bloody awful as he tried to lick my hand. I have no proof that this was a gipsy turd, but given the proximity to their caravans, I strongly suspect it was!

Our two Balalika x Greenpark Betty pups had a superb rearing with no sickness, plenty of galloping and good fun. The two pups were never injured or hurt at any stage and all augured well for their future racing careers. The bitch (Betty Buttons) appeared to be genuine but had little pace. I say 'appeared' because it can be very hard with some ingenuine dogs to ever really know for sure. If you think otherwise, one day you'll meet a dog that will fool you. It just hasn't happened yet. She qualified easily enough and won a puppy race in a very slow time. Ironically, this race had a couple of dodgy pups in it and Michael Falvey who was the control steward at the time in Navan commented that she looked to be the only one who was actually chasing. We must have sold her after her win as she had no racing future with us but would have done okay at low grade in England where there was more racing. I can't remember selling her though for some reason.

It was obvious the dog (Big Brutus) was something special long before he got to the track. The way he devoured the ground when galloping was a joy to watch. We had some decent dogs in the kennel and we would do hand-slip gallops regularly in the fields, eventually giving everything a head start and slip him behind. The ease of which he could make up the ground against decent race dogs is probably the one thing I remember best about all the experiences I had over many years. Galloping in a field is of course not the same as winning races on a track, but nonetheless, it was an indication of pace to us in the early days of schooling. We galloped our dogs in different ways. We had access to one hundred acres of the open field opposite our kennels with a gradual uphill slope. We used this with the drag lure and also more often with just one of us walking to the opposite end and waving a flag and shouting the dogs home. This worked well as the dogs would get so excited watching the flag carrier get further away. We always slipped one at a time, so there was a delay between each dog. This ensured that there was no waiting or messing about as some pups will do given the chance. Brutus, as he was affectionately known to us, started well and was well inside the qualifying time the very first time he was put into the boxes. Soon though it became apparent that he wasn't putting the effort in as his times became very variable. This was the only indication as he never looked like he wasn't chasing. Many dodgy dogs can be seen having a look with their heads up, but he wasn't like that. I think only once did I notice the faintest suspicion of this behaviour when he dead-heated for first in the final of a small sweepstake in Navan. He was in front of this race and seemed to wait slightly on the line to enable the other dog to get up to him and tie the race.

He was the biggest, single disappointment I had in greyhounds. In trials, he usually tried more than when racing. There was a dog we took from someone to train called Long

Island Lad who had been badly trained and was overweight and not in good condition, although he was very genuine. He had just turned two years old. When we got him cleaned up and some weight on him and fit, he started to show a lot of ability. This dog later broke the TR at Mullingar, trained by us over 600 yards, but more about this later. Brutus always ran well against this dog for some reason and seemed to dislike him and always tried against him. The two of them started doing very fast clocks at Navan from the time Brutus was about sixteen months old. We never took Brutus to Mullingar as he was a big gangly dog and we decided the track was too tight for him.

Brutus won a 12-dog graded 525 stakes at Navan in 29.58 where he dead-heated for first. We knew he was an awful lot faster than this. A couple of runs later he came from about nine lengths off the pace at the third bend to win going away in 29.26 (TR 29.04). He did nothing in this race until for whatever reason decided to chase home. Around this time, we took him and Long Island Lad for a private trial on a Saturday morning and Brutus beat him by three lengths in 28.78. This run was nearly four lengths inside the track record and meant that both dogs were inside it. The hare driver Dermy Casserley made a point of popping his head out of his box and commenting on it being a fast run. We pretended we hadn't clocked it and he said that going by the speed of the hare it was about 28.80. He bettered this to 28.70 a couple of weeks later. It was well known at Navan that if you had something good, other people would soon know about it. It was also known that for a few quid the surface would be running at its optimum on any race night. This meant the track on these nights would be flying, very useful for selling a pup that had won in a fast time. But, on Saturday morning trials the track would be back quite a bit as it was never watered before a trial session. A 28.80 run on these conditions would probably result in a 28.60 run when the track was at its best.

Thus, it was a well-known fact at Navan that Brutus wasn't genuine. Some races he would just tag along at the rear of the field and make no effort, others he would decide to chase late on. We decided to try and break the track record with the dog at Navan officially on race night, just to have it on his card and give us more options with the dog. So, one Thursday night when he was about 21 months old the stage was set. A good five dog field was assembled and the hare started its run. I remember being so excited, which was short-lived. The traps opened, but Brutus had turned at the last moment and was facing the wrong way when it mattered and his chance was gone. The dog never did that ever at any other time, even as a beginner. I didn't think too much into it at the time as I was very disappointed. Here I had a dog that was more than capable of not only breaking but smashing a track record to bits and he was facing the wrong bloody way! Later on though, upon reflection, I think there was something put inside his box that night to make him turn. Some food product like honey perhaps that would stick easily. The dog was so greedy he probably would have tried his best to get at it despite the approaching hare, given his propensity for on-off chasing. The track record was broken alright in this race in 28.88 by a son of Daleys Gold who had been regularly racing at Newbridge and Shelbourne Park. This dog was brought in I do not doubt to hopefully spoil our night. To my knowledge, this dog never raced at Navan before or afterwards either. Navan was like that. Full of begrudgery and people who hated to see anyone do well or have anything good. A lot of Irish have this mentality. Maybe it's a bad strain that applies to all nationalities, but it's rife in Ireland.

If Brutus had chased that night and was beaten by the dog that broke the record, I'd have had no problem with that. But as far as I'm concerned, certain people were determined it wouldn't be our night and it wasn't! I also believed that he was at least three or four lengths better than the clock that night.

We often gave our track-bred pups a run up the coursing field, but only the ones we knew could run a bit or sometimes in a bid to awaken their chasing instinct. We certainly didn't run every pup up the field. Brutus was such an exception and he showed amazing speed. At the Ballyjamesduff (Cavan) coursing meeting, we asked the slipper to give us a shout when there was a bye course to run him alongside a dog that would otherwise be having a solo run. This doesn't always happen of course but on this day, we were lucky and he called me shortly afterwards. He warned me though that the dog he would be running against was favourite to win the all-aged stake that day. Brutus beat the experienced dog easily, despite losing lengths at the start due to his inexperience. The dog he beat made the final of the competition that day, beaten much less easily than Brutus had beaten him. This prompted us to enter him in one of the last remaining Derby Trial stakes that guarantee a place in the Coursing Festival every February in Clonmel.

We ended up selling the dog beforehand though. Danny Reilly was a local businessman who owned several greyhounds and he called into our paint shop to discuss buying the dog. He knew all about him and his penchant to chase or not chase depending on his mood, courtesy of Dermy Casserly the hare driver at Navan. He knew about his private trials and the times he'd done and he still wanted the dog. I said that we'd tried everything to get him to chase and he replied that where the dog was going in England he was certain to get him going properly. I smiled and wished him the best of luck. He paid £2500, which was too good to refuse for a dog nearing two-year-old, dodgy as he was.

I told him about the Coursing Stake that the dog was entered in and that he should run him as the fee was already paid and he had his place. We knew he would try 100% on the live bunny. I even offered to keep him and run him in it for him as he didn't train any dogs himself, but he wasn't interested. He was full of excitement and promise that only a flying machine can bring if he got him going right as he believed he could. I told him he'd likely win the Coursing Trial stake and qualify for Clonmel, but he wanted to send him across the water as quickly as possible.

About six weeks later he popped into the shop and asked if we wanted to buy the dog back for £500! He should have coursed the dog where he would always have ran gamely and really tried.

I didn't breed Greenpark Betty again after the second litter, such was the frustration and despair that those pups created. The pace they had was terrific, yet something in their genetic makeup was seriously amiss. A local guy expressed an interest in breeding her again to our stud dog North Line and I let him take her. They were no better than the first lot.

In hindsight, I now regret that I didn't put her to a pure Coursing bred sire for another litter and concentrate on coursing them and keep them away from the tracks altogether. But to do this she would have had to been ready for mating in November or early December to ensure January or February pups. I guess the reason I didn't was that the litter would have had little commercial value and I'd have had to keep and rear most, if not all, of the litter. I'd had too much disappointment, not to mention the time, money and work that we'd poured into those two litters.

Racefield Kate (Game Ball x Raymonds Pride)

Racefield Kate or Maggie as we called her, was a black bitch with only a couple of trials on her card. She was unraced due to problem toes, I was told. She was bought on the strength of her breeding as she was a litter sister to double derby winner Make History. She would have raced at about 60 lbs. She was low to the ground and a slightly stocky bitch without much leg to her.

The first dog we mated her to was crack sprinter Strange Dilly who was the by-dual classic winner and decent stud dog The Stranger out of Dillydontdalley who won a very good Produce Stakes over 525 in Clonmel, beating our stud dog North Line who was hot favourite to land the final. She led up, he found early trouble and started to catch her but found the finish line came too soon!

Strange Dilly was a muscular, good looking fawn dog who had won an astonishing 42 open races in England from 64 starts and broken two track records, one of them at top London track Wembley. He'd raced at 70 lbs and was handled at stud by Ned Curran in Urlingford, Kilkenny. Ned Curran at this time must have been pushing eighty years of age and his son Arthur was handling the dog under dad's supervision. Ned had previously handed great stud dogs of the past such as Yellow Printer and Printers Prince.

Strange Dilly wasn't long at stud and as is the wont of sprinters, he wasn't a proven sire nor was he well patronised. My Da was a big fan of early pace and when I suggested the dog and told him of his racing record, he was all for us using him. Despite the dog being an out sprinter who was at his best at around 300 yards, I loved the way the dog was bred most of all. His sire had won the Irish Leger and the Laurels over 550 and 525 yards respectively and his dam won her classic over 525, so the dog was bred to be a middle-distance runner, despite him turning out to be a pure out and out sprinter. He was certainly bred to be a champion and any dog who wins 42 opens has to be very genuine and honest.

We also didn't believe in spending large sums of money on stud fees. At this time, we believed that it was a numbers game. To make it a successful sire, any dog needs a certain number of bitches. We knew that a lot of the so-called top sires had simply served many more bitches and any fool knows that the more runners a dog has running usually equals more winners. How can any dog make it without a certain number of runners? Nowadays, I don't have such a clear-cut view but still maintain that no stud dog can make it without a decent number of quality bitches. It's only when they get these proven dams and fail to produce well to them that they can then be labelled a failure. A great many young dogs never get that chance.

Nowadays, a mating that produces no pups will result in a full or partial refund with most stud keepers. In 1992, this was not the case. If the bitch had no pups, you got a return service that was somewhat ironically always labelled as a 'free service to missing bitches' with the implication that the failed mating was solely the bitches fault and the stud fee that you paid was for the stud dog serving the bitch regardless of whether the coupling was successful or not! It's ridiculous to think of this now, but that's the way it was. No mention was ever made of the numerous dogs who were knowingly firing blanks by their stud keepers or from the ICC (Irish

Coursing Club) who profited from every mating, successful or not.

The fact that Strange Dilly was newly at stud and an unknown quantity as a stud dog didn't matter to us. We believed Maggie (Racefield Kate) was a decent brood bitch. There was another dog newly introduced at stud called Chet who was an American import. I really liked his breeding too and was torn over whether to go to him or Strange Dilly. Chet was standing at stud with Pat Dalton's son Michael in Golden, Tipperary and ended up doing very well from limited opportunity. He produced mainly strong staying types. There had been many American stud dogs brought into Ireland on the back of the legendary Sandman, but none of them had anything near the success that the little white and black dog had. American dogs were somewhat viewed with suspicion as very few of them proved to be any good. Those that did have some success usually had a mix of American and Irish blood in them, like Sail On II who was a decent dog. I did speak to Michael Dalton about using Chet and he assured me that the dog would not have been sent to Ireland if he wasn't top class. He offered me the use of the dog for £100 (half his usual stud fee), but I decided to use Strange Dilly instead, who I got for the same £100 fee. To put this into perspective, the top 5 sires at this time were priced between £750 and £1000. It didn't matter whether you paid £100 or £1000 if you got no pups the same 'free service' rule usually applied and it was mainly for this reason we rarely sought the top sires. It's easier to stomach the loss of £100 than £800 - £1000.

Most Irish breeders will not consider using a pure sprinter at stud under any circumstances. Their biggest fear is pups that don't stay, although there's never a guarantee what distance you're going to get from any blood cross. There's a son of Brett Lee at the time of writing at stud for free in Ireland called Ela Ela Genie who was a great sprinter. His breeding though (like Strange Dilly's) suggests middle distance through both sire and dam and his litter brother won the Consolation Final of the Irish Derby over 550. A sister was also top class over 525, yet he has to be offered for free because he's a sprinter and thus faces prejudice for it. I would think there's a big chance that this dog will produce sprinters and middle-distance stock, but unless he gets a wonder dog from his early, limited mating's, his chance of getting the patronage his ability and breeding deserves is minimal.

I drove down to Urlingford for the mating to Strange Dilly and the dog mated the bitch that night and again the following morning as I stayed the night in a local B&B. I was going out with a girl at the time (now my wife) and I had promised to phone her at a certain time that evening to the phone box nearest her house in Trim Co. Meath, as her Mother had no phone. The first mating done, Arthur Curran took me to a nearby pub for a pint after the bitch was fed and kennelled for the night and I completely forgot to ring Linda, who was waiting for ages outside the phone box and wondering had something happened to me. No one in Ireland had mobile phones in 1992.

The next morning, I went into a local shop in Urlingford and bought a scratch card and won one hundred quid, the price of the stud fee. I took this to be a good omen.

The litter of ten pups were born in July 1992 and were very even in size and strength. All blacks and fawns, there was eight bitches and two dogs. We decided to keep both dogs and two of the bitches. As they grew, we realised they weren't the biggest pups, although they were fit and healthy and happy in themselves. Normally pups are advertised at twelve weeks of age, but we waited until they were five months before advertising them (as they were on the small side) in the Sporting Press at £175 each. I advertised them cheaply as I knew Strange Dilly pups wouldn't be sought after as he both a sprinter and wasn't a proven sire at this time. The bitch also had only a couple of winners at this time and nothing exceptional.

We sold four of them from the advert, one went to Dublin, two stayed locally and one went to Monaghan. The litter had a superb and trouble-free rearing and they used themselves and galloped hard every day they were let out of the paddock into the big field. They used to single out one bitch who always proved very difficult for the others to catch as she would take off on mazy runs when they hunted her and often they couldn't get her. She was very noticeable when she did this and we decided she was a keeper. She turned out to be the best bitch in the litter. Her name was Racefield Dilly.

Later on, the other two bitch pups, both fawns, were sold at around ten months of age. The smaller one of the two was named Vercingetorix and was bought by two brothers from Navan, one of whom was a friend of mine. She was their first greyhound and their last. She was trained by us until later sold.

She was very small, actually the smallest bitch in the litter (and none of them were very big) and raced at only forty-seven to forty-eight pounds weight. She was also quite short in length and looked more like a big whippet, but she could run like the wind given her size. I didn't want her race card to show she was quite so small and always leaned on her a bit on race nights to push the scales to show fifty pounds. I knew the two brothers that owned her were keen to sell if she would make any money and any bitch that showed less than fifty pounds weight would be nearly impossible to sell, such is the stigma against small greyhounds.

In fairness, this 'size stigma' is often justified. Very few bitches under fifty pounds in weight win races and very few dogs under sixty pounds are any good either.

Vercingetorix won her first two races in Mullingar, one over 325 and one over 525. The litter in general, with one exception, didn't get 525 yards at top pace, but it was only in the top company this was apparent. They all quickly developed good trapping ability and clever track craft. Every one of them railed tightly yet could run from any box, which was a big thing as there was no seeding in graded races in Ireland at this time. Only the top competitions allowed seeding, so a lot of races were spoiled by dogs that needed out coming in and dogs that needed in coming out.

Then she lost two races after being bumped up in the grading and was down to run in another sprint in Mullingar. I remember this night well. I was working in the shop in Navan and after closing up had to rush back to the kennels, feed and let out the other dogs and get the bitch ready to go to the track. I can't remember where my Da was, but he wasn't around. I gave the bitch a quick rub down and got her racing jacket and muzzle and put her into the van and set off on the forty-minute drive to Mullingar. There were two gallons of paint in the back that should have been taken out earlier but had been mistakenly forgotten about in the rush. Suddenly, a driver in front rammed on his brakes and I followed suit, with the result that the paint cans flew forward with one going over on its side and cracking open, splattering the wee bitch. This wasn't your ordinary emulsion waterborne stuff, but the kind used for milking parlour walls and floors; a thick rubber and highly toxic synthetic oil paint. You couldn't pick a worse type of paint to get on a dog, who then jumped over the seats in beside me, giving me some as well. My van at this time was a Ford Transit that didn't have a bulkhead to split the cabin in the way vans of today usually do.

We got to the track without further mishap and all I could do was wipe off any paint that was sitting thickly on the bitch. I couldn't get the paint stains off her though as to do that required synthetic thinners and I didn't have any in the van. Water was useless as it would be with any oil product and white spirits that I did have with me wouldn't do the job either.

My girlfriend Linda suggested we just withdraw the bitch from the race but there was no way I was doing that after busting my arse to get there. We did get some funny looks and stares as we walked in and if I had been interested I probably would have seen a smirk or two from some quarters, but I made my way in as if nothing untoward had occurred. I gave the bitch time to empty as I made my way over the inside of the track to the weighing room. Waiting in line to weigh in, I could see everyone staring at the paint and a couple of people I was friendly with asked what happened and that was it. The control steward Gerry Leech made a bit of a joke about it that was so unfunny I've forgotten the words.

The weigh-in over with, I kennelled the bitch and went to get something to eat, somewhat glad that much was over with. We were running in the fifth race at about nine o'clock, so had an hour and a quarter approximately to kill before I'd go and get her ready. As I made my way to get her, I remember wondering if the paint incident would affect her at all as she did get enough of a fright to warrant her jumping up into the front of the van.

I put her lead on her and fitted her jacket and muzzle. The jacket covered a good bit of the paint but you could still see a bit of it around her neck and head. I noticed Weasel McQuaid, as we called him, sniggering and gesturing at the bitch to one of his friends as I was walking her around waiting on the steward to call time. Weasel McQuaid lived outside Kells about a mile and a half from our kennels. He attended both Navan and Mullingar tracks regularly, particularly Navan where I knew he supplied information to one of the bookmakers there. At first, he appeared friendly, but I quickly realised he was only on the make and looking to find out what we had coming on in the kennel and quickly gave him and his like short shrift. The name of Weasel suited him as he looked like a human weasel, small and sly. He didn't work and I knew he was on disability benefit, despite the fact there was nothing wrong with him but laziness. He was also renowned for making claims and had numerous 'falls' over the years.

I was furious that he was standing there openly laughing in front of people. "What are you laughing at?" I asked. "Look at the state of that bitch" he retorted.

"Why don't you go and make a claim," I said, making sure everyone in the vicinity heard.

His face turned bright red and he stormed off raging.

The bitch took a flyer from trap four and won by five lengths in 18.92 which was the best of the night.

I can't remember the reason why now, but the two brothers that owned her weren't at the track this night, so I got the video man to put the race onto a VHS tape.

Vercingetorix alternated between the 325 and 525 at Mullingar. The track suited her as it was the tightest track in Ireland and if you led into the first bend, you often left trouble behind, so it suited dogs with track craft and early pace. But, small as she was, she had genuine pace and trialled well at Navan too, which was much more of a galloping circuit. She'd won five from eleven races and been in the first three on eight occasions. In these times, the entry fee was £5 and you got £50 when you won a standard race and between £8 and £10 for second place, depending on the track. Tracks paid out on the night in cash. You got nothing for third.

When she'd been beaten and found trouble in a couple of races in a row at Mullingar and we decided to switch her to Navan. The Byrne brothers that owned her were reluctant to race her there as they were from the town and thought it would be embarrassing if she didn't win. This shows how naïve they were; unsuited to greyhound ownership. Finally, I persuaded them that a change of track would probably do the bitch some good.

There was another reason for wanting to switch as well. Officially Navan was at the time rated half a second faster than Mullingar over the 525, so a dog winning in 30.00 at Mullingar would be graded 29.50 at Navan (in theory anyway). We knew that these times didn't bear true in reality, especially in winter where the grass at Mullingar could be waterlogged and be running a full second slower. We had a lot of success in switching winning dogs from Mullingar to Navan, in particular.

'Vercingetorix' best time at Mullingar at this time was about 30.25, which should be equal to 29.75 at Navan. She was much better than that.

I remember one of the brothers, Noel, (whilst I was friends with his younger brother Martin) whom I could only tolerate in small doses, made a comment, "It's about time she won again". My Da just looked at me and I reminded Noel that in racing, it's considered that if you average one win in six races you're doing okay. To win nearly 50% moving up in grade with every win as anyone with any sense knows is a rare deal.

So, this night in March the bitch was running in her first 525 race at Navan. It was a freezing cold night and there was talk of imminent snow forecasted. She took a flyer from the traps and won by ten lengths in 29.54, which at this early point in the season was the fastest time of the year. She was eight lengths clear halfway down the back straight when Noel asked me if I thought she would hold on! I pretended I hadn't heard him. She was nineteen months old at this time.

This win delighted the two brothers who felt they'd lose face in defeat and they had a fair few quid on her as well. But, they had no real-time or love for the dog or for the racing itself. They were more interested in horseracing, but not being able to afford a horse, had become reluctant owners of a greyhound instead. The saying a greyhound is 'a poor man's racehorse' was certainly true in their case. The dog for them was only a means to an end and when a local agent approached me a couple of days after this latest win, we all sat down and discussed it. The agent was Michael Kearney, a native of Navan who frequented both Navan and Dundalk tracks, looking for dogs to buy on behalf of connections in England. A few years later he got to know Nick Savva well and was instrumental in making the latter's travel arrangements when he would bring dogs over for the Dundalk International race. I found him pretty straight if a little greedy, but then most agents are. He had a stud dog around this time called Easy Silver who was a strong staying type dog who ran all distances from 525 to 810 yards. The dog was beautifully bred (Sole Aim x Tidy Colina) and his dam, in particular, had produced many top-class offspring. He promoted the dog extremely well and got over fifty mating's, although few of them would have been to top bitches. When the mating's slowed down as always happens sooner or later, he sold the dog to stand at stud in Scotland. The first pups hit the tracks in Ireland and were sensational. Many of them were sold for big money and Michael tried to buy the dog back but was unsuccessful.

He offered twelve hundred pounds for the bitch, who's record was now six wins from twelve starts. I put this offer to the two brothers and they asked me what I thought. I knew they wanted to sell her but what they were asking was if the money was enough.
"If you intend to sell her, you should probably sell her now," I said
"Will she not be worth more if she improves?" Noel said.
"She's already improved a lot and she may or may not find more improvement. You have to balance that with the fact that she's getting older as well and once she's two years old her value will drop very quickly from then on.
If you want to keep her and enjoy racing her, she'll pay her way and win her share of races as long as she remains sound, but it's your decision."
"What do you think of the amount offered?" said Martin who was the more astute of the two by far.

"It's not great," I admitted, "but she's a very small bitch and they're always difficult to sell. Overall, you're doing pretty well at twelve hundred. She cost 175 and she's won about 350 in prizemoney as well, so she doesn't owe you anything". Not to mention the fact they'd backed her four times and collected each time.

They always wanted to sell, I knew that but also knew they were suspicious enough to wonder if the price was fair and if they were being short-changed. They probably wondered if my Da and I were getting something out of it, although it was never said and we weren't.

So, the bitch was sold for £1200 and the brothers took the bitch to Michael Kearney themselves and collected their money. I reminded them to bring back the lead, which was ours. Michael Kearney called into the paint shop a few days later and was moaning about the fact that there was no lead with the dog, but I wasn't long about putting him straight on the fact that the lead was mine, the dog wasn't. He told me the bitch was going to some trainer he dealt with at Wembley where the standard trip was 490 metres. I told him she that was too long for her and a smaller, tighter track would be best. This was later borne out by the fact she didn't prosper at Wembley, but when moved to Portsmouth and the 438-metre distance, she made the top grade and won many races there.

The two brothers paid the remainder of their kennel bill that was only about a hundred quid and gave us nothing extra. It's customary for the trainer to get 10% when they sell a dog for an owner, but not this time. Despite the luck and money, they got with their first greyhound, it was also their last.

The two dogs in this litter to Strange Dilly were named Our Steve and Stranger Still. Our Steve was fawn in colour and never raced due to something wrong with his pelvis that meant he could only run on three legs. He was born with this and it wasn't apparent that he was effectively a cripple until he was about seven months of age and only noticeable running at speed. Nonetheless, we tried him to see the extent of the defect and he was well inside qualifying time and would have been capable of winning low-grade races, but there was no point in that and him finishing lame all the time. He was a very determined dog and mad keen and it was a pity he was as he was.

Stranger Still - the black dog was the fastest in the litter. He was only sixty-two pounds racing weight, but this didn't deter him in any way. He was single-minded, very genuine and found a lot of improvement in schooling. He didn't get the hang of trapping as quickly as his smaller sisters but had more pace than them all round. They could sometimes beat him in very early trials simply because he missed the break often in his early attempts.

He won his first race at Navan in 30.10 for 525, which was a poor time for him as he was a hell of a lot faster than that. For him to win that night gave us a glimpse of what was to come as he missed his break, found himself bumped out at the first bend and came from last at the second bend to win by six lengths. Michael Falvey, the control steward, remarked to me that he was a very fast dog. We knew that and decided to shift him to Shelbourne park to see how he would run against better opposition and also because his slow win at Navan meant he'd be graded well anywhere he went. In Dublin, though, grading often meant little as the best pups in the country started there.

Shelbourne Park didn't really suit him although he won two races in a row there in 29.87 and 29.81, leading the way in one and coming from behind in the other. I think the 525 trip there was too stiff for him and he tired badly in the run home. I also think sand suited him better than grass, which Shelbourne was at this time.

We decided to race him in Mullingar as he'd trialled there and was doing fast clocks. He was still much better than his card suggested on paper and we reckoned there was a race to be won at Mullingar. There was a guy called Declan Kelly that owned a schooling track near Tullamore and he was a prick, but my Da had a certain weakness for some people and he offered him a 'tablet' that would supposedly enhance the dog's ability and ensure he would trap well, which could be a bit erratic. The dog got his tablet and money was placed with the bookies and the hare started to run. The dog broke badly, was last going into the first bend and ran smack into the inside rail at the first bend. Whatever effect the tablet had it must have affected his eyesight. What was in the tablet I've no idea, but it was clear that rather than enhance the dog's ability, it suppressed it.

No doubt the fella who gave the tablet had a right laugh at our expense, but it was a good lesson. Never again, would we use any type of tablet on any other dog. Luckily enough, the dog wasn't injured and was fine afterwards.

We switched him back to Navan shortly after this and he won from trap to line by ten lengths in a super 29.22, which was the fastest time of the night by far. We decided to sell him on that run as we still had his sisters and other pups coming through, so time and space were at a premium.

Although Navan suited him and Mullingar and Longford probably would have too, Shelbourne Park was too stiff for him and he would never have been anywhere near top-class there.

He'd won four races from eight starts and we sold him for £2200. He went to Stainforth where the standard distance was 483 Metres and probably too much for him. He was eventually switched to one of the other London tracks and ran in top grade and minor open races.

Dillydreamer - this bitch was a little bigger than most of her sisters and raced at fifty-four pounds. She won her first race at Mullingar, out and gone winning by six lengths in 30.40. She went to England after this and only had this one race with us. I remember her and Vercingetorix used to trial together and two more even bitches I've never seen. There was always only a length at most between them and it was a toss-up as to who would win every time they ran against each other. Seeing how decent the much smaller Vercingetorix improved with experience, I'm sorry I didn't hold onto this bitch.

Racefield Dilly - this black bitch was the fastest and best bitch in the litter. You might remember me saying earlier how her littermates as pups used to chase and try to hunt her whilst running loose in the fields and she'd twist and turn and more often than not, elude them. She was only fifty pounds in weight but was racy looking for one so small. We took her to Shelbourne park one night early in her early days and she won in the waterlogged grass in a slow time that was officially rated half a second slow (in reality it was probably a second slow). She was led up in the race and hit the front off the second bend and won handily enough. She liked Navan track and won a lot of races there, the best in 29.38 for 525 and won an open heat of the Barry Cup over 550 in 30.78. She stayed better than any of her comrades. She couldn't match the early speed of her brother (Stranger Still) but would have beaten him over 550, which was her limit distance wise. Her extra staying ability meant she had a bit extra if she didn't lead and often came from behind to win. For some reason, we sold her to Bev Heaton, a contract trainer at Bellevue in Manchester, along with one of her sisters (Dillydreamer). Both bitches won races but Dilly didn't settle as she only made middle grade there and she came back to us about six months later with a sore wrist. I can't remember now why I let her go there at all. I can only think that we had so many pups coming through and that was the reason why, and she went with the proviso that she came back to us for breeding when finished racing. She settled back in as she'd never been away and after a lay off started winning regularly again for us. Now and again, she'd get a little 'wristy' and need laying off, but she continued to win regularly. She was remarkable in many ways. She could finish a race holding her wrist (often having won) and be laid off for three or four weeks with no galloping whatsoever and go straight back to the track and win again. All dogs are different in what they need to get and keep them fit, but she was the most naturally fit dog I ever had. At the time I kept track of her races and she raced until she was four years of age and won at least twenty-five times. I don't know the exact number as I was unable to find out with certainty how many races she won during her time in England. She certainly was no contender for the Oaks but I'd gladly take her like again over and over. She was very soft-mouthed for a greyhound and often caught the odd rabbit in the field but wouldn't harm it, yet was as hard a chaser as I've ever seen.

Her first litter were to Alpine Minister who was making a name for himself as stud dog at the time. He was standing with Martin Tucker just outside Longford. Martin has had several stud dogs in his time but suffers from his location and the ignorance of many Irish breeders, who will not travel outside the most heavily populated greyhound counties of Tipperary, Limerick, Cork and

Kerry. He has always struggled to get both quantity and quality bitches for his stud dogs (as I would too later on). Martin later invested in a top-class rearing facility and that's what he concentrates on today. He's reared many top-class dogs and is a nice fella. I always found him good to deal with and a straight talker.

This litter was a little disappointing. They were very genuine, but few of them showed any early pace to get excited about and only Racefield Pirate showed any promise. He won first time out in Navan in 29.80 and we decided to send him to Shelbourne Park sales and see how he got on. He won a good trial there in 30 secs but failed to meet our reserve on the bench. A man did approach me after the auction but we couldn't strike a deal and I took him home. The man came back to me a day or two later and we sold him for £1250. He was eighteen months old. We didn't keep him as we liked early pace in a dog regardless of his grade. Our philosophy was always that early pace wins races, out in front often leaves trouble behind and gives the best chance of winning when graded fairly and the dog although young didn't have enough early pace for us.

There was a dog recently introduced at stud at the time called Ayr Flyer who had been a prolific open race winner in England and also Ireland. He won the Dundalk International Invitation and was runner up in the English Derby final to the great Moral Standards. He also made the final of the Irish Derby. He had great early pace and was a well-bred son of the very fast (and unlucky) Ardfert Sean, who later sired the hugely paced Irish Derby winner Ardfert Mick. I decided to put Racefield Dilly to Ayr Flyer for a second litter. This litter was much better than her first and all had early pace and some of them had good staying ability too. Racefield Boy won a couple of open sprints for us including breaking 18 secs at Longford for the 330. He also won in Newbridge over 300 in a good time as well. We sold him to England and he raced at Bellevue over the 465m trip but he wasn't suited to it and only attained A3 there. One of the litter we sold as a pup was a bitch called Baconstown Dilly who despite being very small (50lbs) won several races from 525 to 750, culminating in a 42.90 win at Newbridge for 750 that merited a rating from greyhound data (which was new to implement this rating scale) of 100.

Racefield Dilly was leased out to friends of ours but was killed shortly after in a kennel fight.

Magnolia Julie - This was a fawn bitch who initially you might remember was supposed to have been sold at five months of age, but the fella refused her as she had a 'fat' toe on one of her back legs. This should have been an omen that we were to keep her, but we had lots of dogs to look after and pups to school and we ended up selling her as a ten-month-old sapling for £300. It was a bad decision.

A fella called Noel Donnelly bought her. He owned one of the first video rental shops in Navan town and made a lot of money out of it for several years before the chain stores like Extra-vision gained a foothold and started affecting his business. He was a Londoner, probably from Irish parents and he was a lazy sod, who always seemed to lie about and get others to do stuff for him. He had a brainless son called Les who was one of the most boring people I've ever met in my life. Les seemed to do most of the work with any greyhounds they owned and he hadn't a clue, but thought he knew everything.

We were schooling pups from the litter one Saturday morning and we bumped into Noel and he asked to run his bitch along with her siblings in the one trial, making it a four-dog mock race. We agreed, curious as to what his bitch was like compared to ours. They were about fourteen months at the time and were doing decent clocks for unraced pups. In the trial was Stranger Still, Racefield Dilly, Vercingetorix and Noel's bitch Magnolia Julie. To our surprise, his bitch led into the first bend of the 525-yard trial by at least three lengths. She held this advantage to about halfway down the back straight when the others began to close the gap. They eventually caught her between the third and fourth bend and beat her in 29.80, if I remember rightly. The pups had only been in the traps a few times and were unqualified at this time, so it was a very good run. There were only about four lengths between all four runners and the dog Stranger Still won the trial with Racefield Dilly in second.

My Da knew when Noel asked to run with us that he fancied his bitch and we knew had it been a 350-yard trial over two bends she'd have beaten ours easily in a very fast time. Our pups were very decent with early pace, but his bitch put daylight between her and them in a matter of strides and had real electric early pace. Out of all the pups in the litter, she was the one most like her Daddy Strange Dilly and would be an out and out sprinter.

Sadly. Magnolia Julie failed to realise her potential. She stumbled in her first sprint race in Dundalk when a couple of lengths clear and was probably injured as a result as she didn't race again for some time and didn't live up to expectations. I don't know whether she was genuinely hurt or was just badly trained and maintained. Maybe a combination of both but I do know that her owners were probably the worst she could have had in their ability to get the best from her. She produced a couple of litters but there was nothing of note that resulted in the progeny from the mediocre sires they put her to. I feel she would have been a top-class sprinter with decent training, care and lack of injury.

A couple of years later a story appeared in the Meath Chronicle newspaper and the national Irish Independent paper claiming that Noel Donnelly's video business was a money laundering operation in conjunction with the IRA. I believe this was complete nonsense and Donnelly sued both papers for substantial damages. The case was settled at the eleventh hour on the day of the court hearing for an undisclosed sum, rumoured to have been one hundred grand.

A representative of Noel Donnelly's Solicitor called into the shop one day to ask me a few questions about how I knew Noel, etc. and I thought little about it. A few weeks later, someone else tried to serve me with a summons to appear as a character witness in the afore mentioned trial. I avoided the summons by claiming to be someone else. A sixth sense that day told me something was amiss. Donnelly never asked me if any of his legal team could interview me or if I would be a character witness and I certainly wasn't interested in doing that for someone I barely knew on a personal level, nor particularly liked.

A week after this, the postman arrived with a letter that required a signature. I looked at the letter before I signed, and it looked like a Solicitor's letter from as much as I could see.

I refused it as I correctly deduced it to be a summons to appear in court on his behalf. I can understand that the more character witnesses and people willing to attest to the good character of any individual will increase any subsequent settlement offer, but he had a hell of a cheek trying to coerce me into doing something he'd no right to ask of me (and didn't ask).

Baconstown Dilly & Capri Kate -

these two bitches, black and fawn respectively were bought by John and Carmel Finnegan from Enfield in County Meath at five months of age. We had the two of them back at racing age to get them ready to race by getting them fit and a bit of experience trialling with their siblings. Later on, Carmel Finnegan would take out a trainer's licence and makes her living at that these days and has been reasonably successful. The two bitches were pretty even in ability and both won their share of top grade and minor opens. The fawn bitch won an open bitch race on Cesarewitch final night in 29.25, beating 'Glenholme Lady' who had been a finalist in the English Oaks. This race as was the case with the whole litter, in that with their fast starting, early pace and knowledge of the track, they were able to beat dogs that they really shouldn't have been able to. The bitch made the bend in front and was too far ahead halfway down the back straight to be caught. She was the better of the two but no match for Racefield Dilly or their brother Stranger Still.

Kate No Stranger - was a diminutive fawn bitch who was probably the slowest of all the bitches, yet still won a few races. She too was sold from the advert in the Sporting Press at five months of age and was bought by Kieran Lonergan in Monaghan. Although she might have been slower than her sisters, she was possibly the best brood bitch of them all and definitely left her mark on Irish bloodlines for many years after her time. Indeed, the dam line continues to produce to this day.

Kate No Stranger was mated to a pure sprinter type dog named Farmer Patrick who was at stud in the Midlands and was very cheap to use. Very lightly used, he was regarded as a nonentity in breeding circles and being a pure sprinter didn't help him, married to a bad location as well. He was though, a dog with amazing early pace. I saw a video of him and he led in virtually every race he had, regardless of whether he won or not against the best dogs in England. He raced in all the top events in England up to 480 metres and made the finals of most. In races up to 350 metres, he was seldom beaten. He was also superbly well-bred as a son of Murlen's Hawk (Curryhills Fox x Murlens Toe. Murlens toe was by I'm Slippy x Murlens Chill (sister to top stud dog Murlens Slippy) x Hawkfield Music who was a superb producer from a long line of excellent dams. Curryhills Fox (Bold Work x Lemon Soda) was a litter brother to the great Skelligs Tiger and also Curryhills Brute who was exported to Australia and still shows up in many pedigrees today. Farmer Patrick would have been an excellent stud dog given the opportunity and decent patronage.

I think the litter was decent enough but really can't remember individual details of dogs that I wasn't personally involved with. In this litter was a bitch called Chill Out Olive who later produced Give and Go who won the Irish Produce stakes in Clonmel and a host of other fast dogs. By this time as well the lack of size that was prevalent in

Racefield Kate's pups had gone and Chill Out Olive's offspring and that of her daughters were all decent sized dogs and bitches, wherever the increase in size came from, I've no idea as Kate No Stranger raced at only fifty pounds.

Chill Out Olive produced ten individual offspring that rated above 100 on the Greyhound data form guide that I regard as an excellent tool to evaluate the form of any dog. It's just a pity that records before 2000 are often missing or incomplete on the database.

Chill Out Olive's best producing daughter was Girl with Guitar (Moyne Rebel x Chill Out Olive) herself a finalist in the Irish Oaks. She won at Mullingar in 29.38 and 29.36 and clocked a flying 28.73 at Newbridge along with a 30.07 for 550 at Galway (TR 29.75). She also made the final of the Champion Bitch Stake at Galway. As a brood though she was even better than she was on the track. She produced a host of fine dogs and bitches. Quail Hollow (Royal Impact x Girl with Guitar) won the Cox Cup at Newbridge and clocked 29.61 there for the 550 which was the fast time of the year. He also won the Dundalk International in 2012. He was a superb dog. A bitch Millwards Swaby (Westmead Hawk x Girl With Guitar) broke the track record for the marathon at Crayford over 874 Metres in 56.00 knocking fifteen spots off the record. Steely Passion a daughter of Hondo Black x Chill Out Olive won in Dundalk in 21.31 for the 400 yards and is dam of Vancouver Shea (Tullymurry Act x Steely Passion) winner at Shelbourne Park in 28.24 for the 525. There are many more very fast offspring from this bitch. I've just highlighted the pick of them.

Another daughter Quam Celerrime (Head Bound x Girl with Guitar) has established herself as an excellent brood also, producing flying machines such as Kereight King (by Droopys Maldini) 27.82 Shelbourne Pk for 525 and Racy Thunder to Flying Stanley and many others.

When you look at the top second-generation offspring from Girl with Guitar it's plain to see that the line continues to breed on to this day. Sometimes when you think a line has all but bred itself out, one cross and one bitch is often enough to perpetuate a blood line and ensure its continuity of successful offspring.

Racefield Kate's previous litter to Kyle Jack produced Centreback who won the group 2 Midland Puppy Derby 550 at Mullingar and was runner up in the Irish Laurels final. It's obvious that none of the Strange Dilly litter were of his calibre, yet they were extremely even amongst each other in ability and the litter won far more races than any of her previous or subsequent litters. Some siblings of Centreback won races but they were very ordinary and not prolific winners as were the Strange Dillys. Even the bitches that were second or third string in ability were prolific winners and whilst not top class would win in their grade and often a grade above through their style of running and early pace. The Strange Dilly cross has lived on through the daughters of Kate No Stranger and is still producing, whereas none of the bitches from the Kyle Jack x Racefield Kate litter bred anything of note, nor appear in any second-generation pedigrees of notable hounds. Centreback was too small to get his chance at stud.

For Racefield Kate's next litter, I fancied a dog at stud by the name of Satharn Beo which is Irish for Saturday Live. He was a son of Wise Band and had been making headlines with some very fast offspring. He was standing with Michael Dunne in Portlaoise and the stud fee was 550, which I thought was dear enough. I then heard from someone that his sire Wise Band whom I thought was deceased was very much alive and still serving. Better again, he was only £300 for his stud fee. Wise Band (Yellow Band x Wyse Choice) had won the 1984 Cox Cup at Newbridge and had twice broken the 550-yard clock at Shelbourne Park in 30.23 and 30.18. He had a reputation like many sons of Yellow Band of being a reluctant, but very good sire. The owner assured me if the bitch was right there would be no problem. I took the bitch down to be mated and there were no problems. He was a nice-looking fawn dog, if not overly big and the mating produced nine pups in September 1993. Not bad for a sire that was eleven years of age. Sadly, the litter weren't up to much. They were very keen as regards chasing, but had little ability and were as small as the Strange Dillys had been. We sold a few but kept most of them and this turned out to be a bad decision. Only Tombstone a white and black dog looked like possibly amounting to a decent dog. He won first time out at Navan in 30 secs for 525 and was sold to England at fifteen months. The whole litter ended up racing in England and some of them won races over six and eight bends. Wise Band produced many stayers so this isn't perhaps a surprise, but the problem with stayers is that they seldom show much ability before they're two years old and often it's two and a half before you have anything. They were a big disappointment.

One story that concerns this litter still makes me smile. We brought seven of them at about one year old into Navan one Saturday morning in for their first look at the track and to give them a hand-slip if they showed enough interest. First off, we made the mistake of putting them into the van and leaving their leads on as we usually did with the other dogs. We didn't have our Transit van kitted out with cages as the van also was used to stock our paint business. A couple of miles down the road and we got the pungent smell of dog shit wafting into the cabin. It isn't unusual for dogs unaccustomed to travelling to have a dump or be sick in the back, but by the time we got to the track, not only had they shit all over the van, but they'd chewed the bloody leads as well and what was left of the leads was covered in shit along with themselves from walking it all over the place! You can imagine the state of us bringing them in to the track with a few inches of lead hanging from each collar and the smell to go with it all!

When the Wise Band litter was six months old, Racefield Kate came into season again. We reckoned this might be her last litter or possibly her last chance to produce another decent litter. Of course, we couldn't know at this stage that the Wise Band pups would be a disappointment, but her next litter would be her fifth and she was now eight years old herself. We were still riding high with the Strange Dilly litter and probably should have returned to him for a repeat mating, but decided otherwise. This was probably a bad decision. I tried to book Kyle Jack for a repeat mating to replicate another Centreback or two but he wasn't available. Obviously at this time only natural matings were available.
The dog I really fancied for her was Daleys Gold (Lindas Champion x Ballinderry Moth)

who was an exceptional sire of early pace. The only downside to him as I saw it was that his offspring had a reputation for being very fiery and there were many tales of his pups savaging each other. One other consideration too was he'd only raced at sixty-five pounds and I wondered given her history of having small pups if this was tempting fate. I needn't have worried as he wasn't available either when I rang Michael Dunne about him.

I knew Dunne had an Australian dog just out of quarantine standing in his Portlaoise kennels as I'd saw his two-page spread in the annual greyhound review publication and I have to admit I was intrigued. To be fair to Dunne, he does a brilliant job of marketing his stud dogs with clever and flashy adverts, analysis and statistics that beat everyone else's ads hands down. But an Australian dog! Such a thing was an unknown entity in 1994. Nowadays such has been the success of Australian blood into Ireland that it's almost impossible to find a pedigree today that doesn't have any Aussie blood in it. In 1994, you'd have had the same difficulty finding a pedigree that did!

There had been a few mostly mediocre imports. Aussie Flyer was one such dog who raced his entire career in Europe, mostly Germany and France and whilst he'd been head and shoulders above his opposition, European greyhound racing outside of England, had a poor reputation in Ireland. Many average dogs left Ireland to race in Europe with a lot more success there than they would ever have had in Ireland. I don't know how many bitches 'Aussie Flyer' got, but he had little if any success as a stud dog. I don't know of anyone who used the dog. 'Matthew's World' was another import who was seldom patronised and might have been the very first Australian bred greyhound to stand at stud in Ireland, being a 1980 whelp. The only Australian dog before 1994 to have any real success in Ireland at stud was Meeniyan Prince who sired at least two classic winners in Ballyfolian Shy winner of the National Sprint over 435 at Dunmore and the Irish Puppy Derby winner Crossford Dana over 525 at Harolds Cross. He was at stud with a Galway based vet and I don't know how many bitches he received or anything about him based on statistics. You have to remember at these times there was no internet and no greyhound publications outside of their respective countries and the shoddy publications available in Ireland told breeders nothing worthwhile as regards statistics that would help them in any way to breed better dogs.

Irish breeders simply knew nothing about Australian greyhound racing, nor wanted to. The common consensus and ignorance was that Irish greyhounds (and racehorses) were the best in the world.

Anyway, back to the story. Somewhat tentatively I asked Michael Dunne about the new Australian dog he had and if he was available. His name was Frightful Flash and he was available for the date I wanted.

My Da and I travelled down to Portlaoise on a midweek evening. At this time John Sandman Fitzpatrick was handling all the stud dogs for Michael Dunne and at this time it was still natural matings. Artificial Insemination or AI was somewhat down the line and surgical implants using frozen semen further behind again.

Fitzpatrick was very friendly and the whole mating was trouble free and painless. One thing we always knew when our bitches were ready and the proof of this is that

everywhere we went with a bitch, always resulted in a mating that day and only with two exceptions failed to produce litters, but more about these later. Frightful Flash was a fine looking black and white
dog of about seventy-five pounds in weight. He had a great temperament and was a very enthusiastic worker.

After the mating, Michael Dunne's Dad brought us back to his house where we were given tea and sandwiches by his wife whilst we watched a video of the dog's best races. They were very nice and hospitable people and I was given a tape of the video we'd watched to take home.

There were six healthy pups born from this breeding (four dogs and two bitches) and it quickly became apparent that they were bigger specimens than what Kate usually produced. They weren't huge by any standards but they were noticeably bigger and stronger than her previous litters. They looked really good. Only two other breeders had used the dog since his arrival into the country.

Every imported dog that goes to stud is heralded as a complete outcross, meaning that there is no related blood ancestry. In greyhound circles, there's no such thing as a complete outcross as there will be related blood in any pedigree within twenty generations if not less. Whether common ancestry makes any difference or has any influence beyond six generations is open to opinion as it cannot be proven either way. I'm inclined to think that there can be no influence on a current litter beyond six generations, if not less. The attraction of an outcross is to develop the phenomenon known as 'hybrid vigour'. This is the creation of fitter, healthier and superior offspring through largely unrelated blood. Lurcher breeders will certainly attest to this as they will mix Greyhound, Saluki or Whippet blood with that of working Collies, Terriers and other breeds to create a superior hunting dog with greater abilities than the pure greyhound possesses. These traits include intelligence, greater scenting ability and stamina, if always to the detriment of a slower top speed.

I have seen hybrid vigour occur in many breeds of dog and related hybrids, and it does create bigger, stronger and sometimes superior specimens than more closely related blood ever could. I believe that the more inbreeding that occurs in any dog, the greater the risk of unhealthy and useless dogs. The Australian's have had some success with certain inbreeding lines, but I believe the failures far outweigh the successes and you'll never hear anything about them. I think close inbreeding is a risky business.

The Frightful Flash x Racefield Kate litter were unusual for one reason. Apart from being a bit bigger and stronger than the Irish bred sires she'd been to before, they weren't very genuine. This was very unusual for the dam as to my knowledge every pup she'd had previously chased hard. In my opinion there's only two possible reasons for this: 1. The fault lay with the stud dog, or 2. The blood mix between them produced an unhealthy combination. I favour that the dog was to blame. He later became the champion sire three years running in Ireland and obviously had ability, but I know other people that used the dog and weren't happy with what they got either. This was a decent, proven brood bitch that produced very genuine offspring, regardless of ability. All of her daughters and grand-daughters also produced very genuine offspring. One thing for certain as far as I'm concerned, is that the dog got plenty of bitches and opportunity. The Frightful Flash pups I bred, all had plenty of speed, just their chasing instinct was lacking and a couple of them looked like they were chasing, when they weren't, which is always more heart-breaking when you finally admit to yourself that the bad luck that seems to follow them is of their own making. Dogs can make fools of you especially ones that you've bred yourself. Despite this, a couple of them won first time out (looking all around them) and I believe that the first one to win was Frightful Flash's very first winner in Ireland. They also appeared to have plenty of stamina but it's difficult to assess stamina as anything can stay when it's not trying!

If this litter had been born to Greenpark Betty, I would have blamed her for their lack of genuineness and wouldn't have been at all surprised.

One of them, named Sixshooter, was a black dog that raced at seventy pounds and won first time out in a poor puppy race at Navan in 30.10. Initially, he looked good, after missing his break he ran through the field and took the lead off the fourth bend. But, once he was in front you could see him having a look and although he won, he wasn't really trying once he hit the front. After this, we got a coursing trial for him against another dog, in a bid to boost his instinct. He was well in front but a short slip meant the two dogs got an almighty gruelling trial where they turned the hare multiple times and chased him up and down the field many, many times in a trial that lasted many minutes. The dog he ran with had to receive electrolytes and was rested for six weeks. Sixshooter was full of beans the next morning and showed no ill effects of the previous day whatsoever. Anyone that has coursed track bred dogs knows how much a gruelling chase normally takes out of them. Many people that saw this trial thought the dogs would be fit for nothing afterwards.

Ironically, the night that Sixshooter won his race, there was a fella who had a dog running in the same race whose name was Martin Bogman (name changed slightly) who had a schooling track near Rathangan, County Kildare. He was also a self-proclaimed 'muscle man' for greyhound injuries and usually wore a cowboy hat at the tracks (the irony is not lost on me). My Da, whom I said earlier tended to be impressed by certain people that he ought to have known better about, had arranged for Bogman to check over one of Sixshooter's litter brothers this night. The litter brother Steves Dancer was a black dog with white socks that always looked like he was chasing properly, but seemed to have gone stale after a hugely promising beginning. The dog was in the van and after the race Bogman came out with us and looked at the dog. It was nearing darkness and he started to feel the dog over, moving his hands over the dog's body and I swear I saw him pinch the dog's skin just before he yelped. "There's an injury there" he proclaimed. I just laughed and walked away. I assumed my Da had seen what I had, but when he caught up with me I realised he'd given Bogman the dog to take to his place and 'fix' him. I asked him had he not seen him pinch the dog and he said he couldn't as he was standing in a different place to me. I think above all else he wanted to believe that the dog's bad form had a simple, injury related answer. Needless to say, he wasn't chasing. We collected him two weeks later, supposedly

fixed. The man was paid and the dog was the same as he'd been two weeks previously. There's a lot of so called 'muscle men' in greyhounds. The occasional one has ability, but most of them are chancers and have had no training or study in the subject. I wouldn't mind the latter if they knew what they were doing but few of them are any good and are simply conning people.
We sold two of this litter at three months of age and kept the other four until they started racing. The two we sold were no different as regards their willingness to chase.

Racefield Kate came in season twice a year. When she came in next, the Frightful Flash litter were about four months of age and she looked so well in herself, I decided to mate her one more time. I ought to have gone back to Strange Dilly, but there was another son of The Stranger called Tapwatcher who seemed to be producing excellent offspring, all with great early pace. The dog was standing down the country in Blarney, County Cork about four hours' drive each way with a man named Michael Walsh. I booked the bitch in and drove down on the day. Tapwatcher was a big, leggy, brindled dog who looked every inch a champion. He'd been the best dog by far in the English Derby, but mistimed his start when it mattered and was beaten a short head by Signal Spark, whom he'd easily beaten in prior rounds. The mating went ahead with no hiccups and Walsh complimented me on knowing when the bitch was right and ready for mating. I remember him remarking the many bitches that came and were past the mating day. Due to the distance involved, there was only the one mating possible, as per the case for her previous three mating's. No pups resulted from this mating. I had to phone Walsh and ask him for a refund. He wanted to offer me a return mating, but I told him I wasn't mating the bitch again and due to the distance involved, I wouldn't be coming again. He said he'd get on to the owner in England and sort it out. I had to ring him three times before I got eighty percent of the four-hundred-pound fee back. A year or so later, it became widely known that about 90% of the bitches the dog had received during the last two years of his career resulted in no pups. The dog was clearly firing blanks and his connections didn't see fit to tell anyone. It's easier to say nothing and take the money, I guess.

Changes and Parvovirus

In 1996/97, we started to wind down our greyhound numbers and decided not to breed anymore for the foreseeable future. There were a couple of reasons for this. One reason was that our paint business continued to grow, and we opened an additional shop in the same town (Navan). This meant extra work, and something had to give. Another reason was that we had two litters of pups that contracted parvovirus, even though the mother of the pups had been vaccinated at the six weeks stage and the pups themselves received their vaccinations twice at eight and twelve weeks respectively. Both litters were practically wiped out and the few that did survive didn't amount to anything useful on the track. If you've ever had parvo in your kennels or saw how it rips through pups and destroys them, you know what I'm talking about. If you haven't, then you simply cannot comprehend the suffering and ultimately awful death that follows. The disease simply rips through the immune system of the animal and they've no defence against it. The odd pup can survive it but I've never known a greyhound to be any good after it. There's a smell from the disease that you can never forget after having smelled it.

We asked the vets at the time, what was the point of all the vaccinations when the very thing they're supposed to protect against, strikes anyway! The vets knew this shouldn't have happened and contacted the pharmaceutical firm. They offered us two hundred quid worth of free vaccinations for future use, which my Da accepted. I mentioned this case sometime later to a friend who is a solicitor and he reckoned that they knew the vaccine was faulty or they wouldn't have offered anything. The way the vaccine is supposed to work gives the pups a heavily diluted exposure to the virus, which in turn creates future immunity to it. He reckoned they'd cocked up on the strength of the vaccine and they knew it.

Parvovirus is believed to be airborne and throughout the 1980s and 1990s, it was rampant in Ireland and the UK. If you got it in your kennels, it seemed to linger and once there, it was very hard to get rid of its influence for a long time afterwards. I was very reluctant to breed litters again in the aftermath of this. Plus, the two brood bitches, Greenpark Betty and Racefield Kate were retired by that point anyway and Racefield Dilly had been leased out to friends. The two litters that contracted the parvovirus were from ex-racing bitches sent to us by Bev Heaton who was a trainer at Bellevue in Manchester.

My relationship with my Da was always a stormy one and we didn't see eye to eye on many issues, which only got worse as I got older. At this time, I was about twenty-six or twenty-seven with a child of my own. Although we were alike in many ways, in others we were very different and so were our ideas and opinions. My main greyhound interest was breeding. I loved rearing pups in particular and had a massive interest in bloodlines. He had no interest or understanding of bloodlines and his main interest was in racing and winning races. To give credit where it's due, he was good at training dogs and knowing what they needed to be at their best. He knew instinctively whether a dog was racing too light or too heavy, without trial and error. He was better than me at this.

With the business growing and our lives going in different directions, we decided to have a break from greyhounds for a while. I was married a few years at this stage with one child and in 1999 we wound the greyhound kennel down.

I did follow the scene though and in 2003, I reckoned I had been without greyhounds for too long and decided to buy two pups and ease my way back into the game. I told my Da I was getting back into the dogs again and he wasn't interested in it himself, so I would be going it alone and I was happy to do so. You might remember earlier me talking about a bitch I bred called Sneachta Ban who was by Make History x Rhincrew Exile. She finished third in a bitch stake at Harolds cross, won by a bitch called Fusion (Wise Band x Barneys Girl). A top class bitch herself; she was one of an incredible litter, the star of which was double Cesarewitch winner Ratify who was probably the best dog from 600 to 750 yards of his generation. He proved to be a decent stud dog too from limited opportunities (his strong staying ability seen as a disadvantage to getting patronage). Well, I saw a litter of pups advertised in the Sporting Press by Tom's The Best x Run on Cracker (Right Move x Fusion) who was a daughter of Fusion and a decent 525 runner, if not quite top class herself. The bitch pups were priced at 350 at three months of age and I thought they were the best value in the paper at that particular time of looking.

I had reservations about Toms The Best as he was a son of Frightful Flash, but he'd been a most impressive English Derby Winner and was very unfortunate not to win the Irish one as well. He was a fantastic race dog and was a proven top ten sire even if his progeny hadn't set the world on fire. His best progeny tended to stay on strongly which wasn't unusual given that he had run that way himself. Run on Cracker had won ten races and been a finalist in a couple of good competitions including the Ulster Oaks and her card showed she was extremely genuine. Her previous litter had been decent, so I decided to pick up the phone as they were cheap pups all things considered.

The pups were in Dungannon, about two hours away from where I was living in Cavan and were bred by two brothers, Art and Jim McRory. I had initially phoned Jim from the advert, so it was largely him that I dealt with and both brothers were extremely nice people as is often the case with genuine greyhound folk. I went to view the pups and took my son Iain who had just turned seven at the time. The kennels were very good and spotless, and it was plain to see that the pups had wanted for nothing and were very well done. We picked out two bitches, a black and a black and white. I got twenty euros back luck and he gave my son another twenty and told him to give his sister Kaitlin (born in 2000) half of it. Jim McRory and I kept in touch for a few years after this and he later used one of my stud dogs. About five months later, he called me and asked if I wanted to lease his bitch Run on Cracker as he had enough pups at the time. I took her and mated her to Crack Off who was an early paced son of Mountleader Peer who himself was a son of Tapwatcher and the sire line that went back to The Stranger that I had always liked. This mating only yielded four bitches and although I was quite happy to give Jim a pup from the litter, he wouldn't hear of it as there was only four of them. Unfortunately, despite an all Irish pedigree that looked great on paper, they weren't much good, although they were very keen. Racefield Hitler was the most promising one but got a bad muscle injury in her first race that ended her career. An all Irish pedigree is almost a thing of the past in track-bred greyhounds now, such has been the influence of Australian and to a lesser extent American stud dogs in the last twenty-five years.

Anyway, the two (Toms The Best) pups started me off again in greyhounds, albeit on my own this time. My son, although he liked the dogs, he was too young to be able to help and they were too strong for him. My wife Linda had no interest in the game whatsoever, apart from going racing which she enjoyed. Just before I collected the pups, I spent a week cleaning the kennels inside out with Jeyes fluid and cutting down the vegetation growth in the paddocks. Once the timbers were dry, I gave them a coat of varnish. I also got a new door and new windows fitted as the originals were past it and a few bales of fresh straw in anticipation for the pups.

Widespread internet use has only been a constant in Ireland from about 1999. It had been available for some time before that, but everybody didn't use it or have access to it as they do today. I started using a website called Global Greyhounds that was the first world-wide greyhound forum, it was good as it allowed you to swap ideas and information with like-minded people from all over the world. I was a regular user of this forum and would talk on there about my thoughts and opinions. Greyhound Data later came on stream and quickly took over from Global Greyhounds. It had the advantage of providing a breeding database for virtually all greyhounds past and present (in addition to the forums) and it was a free service, unlike GG which you had to pay to use. Greyhound Data also allowed you to post free adverts to sell your pups and race dogs, which was the first time for Ireland, anyway. We were used to paying a hefty fee for a tiny advert with no pics in the Sporting Press that only appeared once in the paper. Now, we could advertise for weeks with pictures and no limit on words or space and for free!

I became a regular on the forums from 2003 and although it wasn't my intention, people were clearly following what I was putting out there and I started to get asked to rear and school pups for people. These were initially English people who didn't have the facilities to rear and school for themselves and who wanted a decent rearer that they could trust, but also one that would keep them posted and updated as to how their pups were progressing. There were plenty of good rearer's in Ireland then as there are today, but a lot of them were of a certain age that wouldn't be too interested in the internet or providing regular updates by email or any other medium. One of the first people that contacted me and befriended me, if you like, was a Welsh fella by the name of Keith Howells who lived not far from Swansea. He was a very nice fella and we had some great conversations about dogs for many years. He had some pups that needed rearing as he had no facility for that himself. He also offered me a stud dog named Cardigan who was either named after the bay in Wales or somebody's jumper! I never found out which!

Cardigan was from the first crop of Top Honcho offspring. Top Honcho became, in my opinion, one of the best, if not *the* best stud dog Ireland has ever had. He was the next Australian import after Frightful Flash to make the top sire in Ireland and stayed there for many years and was brought to Ireland by Michael Dunne who was also responsible for the former. Cardigan's dam was Queen Panther who produced top-class offspring in every litter, no matter what stud dog she went to and was surely one of the best brood bitches of her era.

Cardigan did not have many races before injury ruined his career. He only ran in the top-class company and was runner-up in the English Puppy Derby final. He'd been a decent, if not the spectacular, performer his breeding suggested he might. He was a poor trapper who never overcame this affliction as many do with time and experience and this blighted his short career.

I was offered the dog for free, just had to pay for his transport from the UK to me and I accepted. I also reared and schooled Keith's pups which he paid me for before they returned to the UK.

Keith Howells is typical of many people in dogs. He had no rearing or training facilities and had to pay for everything, which wasn't easy. Every doggy endeavour he indulged in had to be thought about carefully and budgeted for. Like many people, his dream was to own a really good dog and reap the rewards that are possible from that. Without hopes and dreams in greyhounds, there would be no industry, yet the industry does nothing to support ordinary people and owners.

Cardigan was a big strapping dog of about eighty pounds weight and had a lovely temperament. I didn't really have any broods to suit him and to be honest, I didn't believe in the dog. For me, on the track, he just hadn't done enough or maybe just wasn't quick enough in my estimation. Also, at the time Top Honcho was rising, he hadn't yet made it to the top of the ladder nor yet became the legend he did. Many imports came to Ireland who were probably inferior to Cardigan in terms of ability and breeding that did make it, so I regret not using the dog myself as he was better bred than 90% of the sons of Top Honcho that did make it. He was a better dog than I gave him credit for.

I did advertise the dog for a brief period, initially at 100 Euro per service and free to proven and top-class racing bitches but had no takers. After a few months, I gave the dog to a greyhound breeder who was living a few miles from me to use on her bitches, which she did. In hindsight, I shouldn't have taken the dog unless I was going to use him myself, but I did think I'd get a few breeders willing to use him and if I'd had a bitch to suit him, I would have. I've no doubt that had he gone to one of the top stud kennels, he'd have got lightly used and had some sort of a chance to establish himself, but there remains in Ireland, a prejudice away from the leading stud kennels and it's very difficult to establish a new dog as I would later find out on a few occasions.

The two Tom's The Best pups had a good rearing with no sickness or injuries and one of them, in particular, was very racy looking and eye-catching (Racefield Dixie) and when first taken to the track for a hand slip, they both were mad for it.

When you have nothing in the kennel to trial with or judge a run against, dogs will make a fool of you. You don't know how to judge the going if you're only having the one run, and the going can vary by twenty or thirty spots over 525 on different days. You don't know where the dog is doing his best work, or if it has any early pace. The only thing you can tell is if the dog is struggling to get the distance. This was the position I found myself in with these pups as I had nothing else in the kennel to compare against or run them with, unlike in previous years when spoilt for choice.

When I hand slip pups for the first time, I let them watch a few trials beforehand from the middle of the inside of the track. Usually, you'll get an indication of interest, but not always. You get the odd one that follows it with their eyes but shows no excitement or wanting to go after it. You're hoping to see some sort of interest. Then I used to walk the dog up to the halfway point between the first and second bend, so they begin on a bend and then have the long straight immediately afterwards. If you start them on a straight, many will lose sight of the hare on the first bend and you certainly want to avoid that. I always used to tell the hare-driver too that they were first-timers, so he would moderate the hare speed. I'd always use the sprint distance wherever I was and usually no more than 300 yards for a first slip.

It became obvious soon after that one of them was about six lengths better than the other. They were named Racefield Dixie and Racefield Best, with Dixie being the faster. She was inside qualifying time for the 525 at Mullingar first time she was put in the traps, with her sister about three lengths off qualifying time.

I decided to bring them in and make their next trial an official one and qualify them. I made a mistake with this as Dixie won the trial in 30.54 for the 525 at Mullingar (qualifying time 31.20), which was an improvement of half a second from her previous run. Mullingar track is rated half a second slower than the other tracks, so it was rated 30.04 anywhere else. I didn't expect that much improvement in a week. They were fifteen months old. There were plenty of puppy races won in similar times to this and it meant she'd be harshly graded, on paper anyway for her first race. I should have galloped her well before the trial and given her a bit of grub, but she surprised me.

You've six weeks between when a pup qualifies and has to race, or you need to requalify. What I liked to do was get a pup qualifying as soon as possible after they'd been introduced to the traps. This depends on the individual ability of any dog, but usually, you'll find at least half a second between qualifying and racing for the first time. I would leave the card into the track after four weeks, which gave the racing managers two weeks to put the dog on the card. Once qualified, they would get three private trials a fortnight, which meant that they'd usually have seven or eight more runs between qualifying and racing, along with greater fitness, better grub and any weight reduction necessary. They'd also be washed, wormed out and vomited with a lump of baking soda.

But, qualifying in 30.54 was too quick. It meant she'd be in with pups or race dogs with more experience and probably a bit older as well. As I said, I had nothing to trial this bitch with other than her sister, who was no competition for her as she'd beat her from start to finish. I did have a feeling though that she was staying on very strongly, which meant she might not be that sharp early on. I just didn't know. One certain thing was that she would likely have to improve quite a bit to win first time out. I decided to advertise her and see if I could get a sale for her. My intention with both bitches was to try and win first time out and move them on, just as had been done with the majority of dogs in the past. I advertised her on the Global Greyhounds (GG) site and a Scotch fella living in Dublin bought her. His username on GG was Tom Burns, his real name was Martin McBride, he told me. He was very secretive and said very little, but he'd messaged me a few times on the forum and contacted me shortly after the ad went up and said he'd have her. The price I advertised was £1250 and he duly paid up with no haggle or quibble. It was a bit strange as he didn't drive and he got the bus to Kells town and I met him off the bus and took him to the kennels, then back to the bus later. He got the bitch picked up by a transporter a few days later. I never heard from the fella again. I know the bitch went to Brough Park initially but didn't feature in her few races there. She then came back to Ireland and started doing better, soon winning in 42.50 over 750 yards. She won a few races in Dublin from 580 to 750 yards and ran in mostly top grades, so she turned out decent enough and fulfilled her early promise. She was later bred from but didn't produce anything of note.

Her sister Racefield Best won a 525 on her fourth outing at Mullingar in a poor time. She ran well though as she was bumped out at the first bend and came from fifth to first, staying on well in the company she was with. I sold her after this run and she became a middle grader in England and won her share from 480 to 722 metres. Both bitches raced at around sixty pounds.

Meanwhile, I had a litter of pups by their dam Run On Cracker to Crack Off at this time, but not much else. I always preferred to breed my own pups, rather than buy them in. I did though make it known on the forums that I was willing to rear pups for people, and the phone started ringing and the paddocks started to fill.

Big Changes a coming

I continued to comment and write on the internet forums and from this, I got a lot of pups to rear. These were mostly owned by UK based people who had bought pups in Ireland from breeders and needed them reared and as is typical, they'd never seen the pups in most cases in the flesh. I did have some Irish owners too, but not as many as the Irish tend to rear their own more often than not.

One of the pups I part reared and schooled before sending back to England was a bitch named Fintans Gwennie who was a lovely looking blue and white bitch and daughter of Droopys Vieri. She came to me at about six months of age and was very keen but didn't show an awful lot on the clock in her early trialling. It just goes to show that some need more time than others. I qualified her at Mullingar over 525 and sent her back to the UK where she would be racing. She ended up an open class staying bitch and classic finalist. She also proved to be a very good brood bitch. Her owner was a Yorkshire man named Jon Knowles who owned her in partnership with his Dad, and they were spot on to deal with and always paid a month in advance, which is a very rare occurrence in greyhounds circles.

I charged 25 euros a week for rearing pups regardless of age and this increased to 40 when they were of schooling age. It's ten years from when I first reared a pup for someone else and prices haven't gone up, but food and expenses have. It's an indicator of how stagnant the game has become.

I've always enjoyed rearing more than any other aspect of greyhounds. Just seeing pups grow, develop and thrive gave me more pleasure than winning races even. I always liked to give pups the opportunity to hunt and get them chasing rabbits and things as early as possible. Unfortunately, rearing alone is almost impossible to make a living from in Ireland and it has to be supplemented by selling pups, schooling and racing. It was at this stage that I started thinking about working with greyhounds' full time and with my internet activity getting me work, it seemed possible to me. Rearing is very poorly paid when you consider that a sapling from five months of age to full growth will eat twice that of an adult dog. Plus, you have to keep them clean, warm and worm them out regularly too, along with the time it takes to look after them. But I was open to doing whatever I needed to in order to work at something I loved.

I was lucky enough to have the kennels and paddocks in place to give it a real go without having to pay rent.

Stud dogs

As I previously said, the first stud dog I had experience with was North Line (Sandman x Cooga Customer). He got about a dozen bitches in his time with us and I got a little experience with working him. He wasn't the best dog from which to get experience with as he was like a bull when he saw a bitch in heat and very difficult to work and control. He was so frenzied that often I had to stop trying with the mating and put the two of them away for a few hours and try again. He used to upset a lot of the bitches too as he would dive on top of them and was so strong he would knock them over. I would learn later on that some dogs would tell you whether or not a bitch was ready by their interest level, but not with this fella as he was intent on action four days either side of them being right. He once ate his way through a shed trying to get to a bitch that was kennelled fifty yards away.

He was the most exuberant (being polite) stud dog I would ever be associated with. He was a gentle giant though and loved people as so many greyhounds do. I had a four-year-old brother at the time and he used to sit on the big dog's back like he was a Shetland pony.

There was another dog that we bought in 1993 for stud purposes. His name was William's Glen and he was a son of I'm Slippy x Tiger Hart who was beautifully bred and a dam of great pace. For those of you that are too young to remember, I'm Slippy was the top sire in Ireland for a few years, and he threw great early pace. His dam line had a touch of coursing blood in it, yet his progeny was notable for being as genuine as they were quick.

There were two outstanding performers in this excellent litter, Boyne Walk and William's Glen, with the former being slightly better. Boyne Walk broke the TR for the sprint at Dundalk and won the Irish National Sprint at Dunmore over 435 yards. He also had success on the coursing field. William's Glen broke the 330 clock at Harold's Cross and was half a length of the 300 clock at Newbridge. He was close to the clock over the 360 at Shelbourne too. He was a semi-finalist in the National Sprint but found the 435 a little stiff for him. A repeat litter a year later produced the very fast Slippy Corner.

William's Glen or Willie as we called him, was still racing at three and a half in Scotland and although past his best, he was still winning races at Shawfield and Ayr. With I'm Slippy being the best stud dog in Ireland, I reckoned Willie could make it as a sire and fancied mating the two broods Greenpark Betty and Racefield Kate to him.

I made enquiries and got the contact details for the dog's owner and agreed to buy him for £3,000. Looking back at it now, I was a bit naïve and with hindsight, I reckon I could have probably got him for a grand less. But, I was young and over-eager, and Graeme Hutt (later to become an NGRC trainer) who owned him made the most of the opportunity. It's important to remember that Boyne Walk had been the most exciting and talked about dog in Ireland for many years and Willie wasn't far behind. He'd even beaten his more illustrious brother over 330 yards. Boyne Walk later became an excellent sire for all distances.

Anyway, I got the ferry from Larne to Stranraer and collected the dog and brought him back myself. He raced at just under seventy pounds and looked every inch the sprinter with a deep chest, strong loins and well-muscled back end. I started advertising him at local tracks only and got very little interest, which I was surprised at. One of my bitches came in season and he showed no interest in her whatsoever. This didn't concern me that much as they don't all take to the stud game like a duck to water. Lots of dogs in training have got a smack when they showed an interest in a bitch, so it wasn't unheard of. I decided he'd benefit from somewhere that would have lots of stud dogs and mating's happening, where he could be introduced to it that way. I contacted Richie O'Regan who had I'm Slippy but he wouldn't take him. I spoke with Jerry Griffin from Sporting kennels on the Limerick/Kerry border and he agreed to take him on a 50% split, less advertising and expenses. I figured if it got the dog going, it was worth it. Griffin had a few stud dogs including the highly regarded Glenpark Dancer and with such kennels, there's often an opportunity for a young unproven dog to pick up bitches when the top sires are booked out, etc.

He only had the dog for about two weeks and rang me to say the dog was no good and wouldn't serve. Not only that, but he'd also sent the dog back with a transporter that morning, giving me no chance to convince him to give the dog more time. To this day, I don't know why he agreed to take him when he wouldn't give him time and a chance. The dog came back and I started galloping him and getting him fit again whilst waiting on one of my broods to come in season and try him again. I had the Strange Dilly litter at this stage just beginning to race and I reckoned he'd be useful in bringing them on. After a few weeks galloping him, I stuck him in a 525 private trial with Stranger Still and Racefield Dilly. The dog didn't get 525, but he'd won an A1 race at Shawfield over the distance a week before I got him. He missed his break and they led him halfway to the first bend when he flew past them and opened up about four lengths between them until the end of the back straight when he started to close a bit. They caught him about fifty yards before the line in 29.40 which was a decent run. He wasn't fully fit and clearly had lost a little of his initial early, but still had great pace. I decided to give him a race or two whilst waiting on him to commence stud duties. He got bumped out of contention in an open sprint and caught on the line, beaten a short head in a decent 525. I waited three weeks, kept galloping him and entered him in another 525 at Navan. I really fancied him to win this and we got half our purchase price back as he romped home at 3/1 in 29.44. (TR 29.10). The dog still had pace but had lost three or four lengths from what he was, so I didn't see the point in running him any further. I did get one bitch mated to him, but she missed. I got the dog checked out by a vet who did some tests and he was deemed to have a low sperm count. As you can imagine this was hugely disappointing as he was bought specifically to that end.

Would he have got bitches? That's a good question and hard to answer for sure, but he wasn't advertised in the press, so I'll never know what interest he might have generated. I do know that he was a dog of the highest calibre and I would have put my bitches to him regardless of whether he ever got another bitch or not. He would have struggled with numbers as County Meath where I was based is not the same as being in the greyhound rich counties of Tipperary, Kerry, Limerick or Cork. His brother Boyne

Walk was always a better bet and he made it as a sire.

Williams Glen was a very primitive type of dog, hunting mad and very determined. I had him out in the field one day and two wild goats had strayed from a couple of fields away into the bottom of the pasture we were in. He spotted them about two hundred feet away and took off. By the time I got there, he'd ripped the throats out of the pair of them. He was okay with other greyhounds though. After this, I only let him off loose in our field where he wouldn't put anything up as once he saw something there was no stopping him.

In Spring 2004, I had only been back in dogs for about a year. By this time, I was rearing over twenty pups and was still working in the business four days a week. I usually spent three or four hours a day at the dogs between early morning and evening times. I was still enjoying the forums and conversing with people there and from that, I got a private message from a guy called Chris asking if he could ring me with a proposition. Chris was a builder from the South of England and he'd recently been in Australia and was looking for someone to manage two stud dogs he'd obtained. The dogs were nearing the end of their quarantine in England and he needed somewhere to place them. I'd never met nor heard of the fella aside from the greyhound forums.

To be honest, it seemed an opportunity too good to be true. One of the dogs had run in the TopGun race over there which is an invitation-only race for the best eight dogs in the country and he'd finished second with Brett Lee behind him and the other dog was an extremely well-bred son of Light Of Fire who was a top Australian stud dog and I was told he'd broken four track records.

Australian stud dogs were very much in vogue in 2004 and they had been popular for ten years and to be fair they've changed the Irish scene beyond what anyone could have foreseen.

I was certainly interested but sceptical that it would amount to anything other than hot air. Firstly, I wasn't a known stud-keeper and why not approach others who were? He probably did and was rejected. Ireland is a very negative place at times and if you're reaching out to someone with an opportunity it's just as liable to be treated with scorn and suspicion as accepted and listened to properly. I'd seen the same thing first-hand with Williams Glen. I did wonder if it was a wind-up.

But, Chris kept phoning and I agreed to take the two dogs. One thing I insisted upon was that he paid for the first round of advertising and promotion of the dogs. If they were getting bitches, then, of course, they could pay for their promotion, and the other stipulation was that I could avail of their services for my bitches without charge.

I met Kenny Walker, the transporter in Enfield in County Meath, early one Saturday morning and collected the two dogs. Their names were Toll Security (Rapid Journey x Sunset Savannah) and Elles Dominator (Light of Fire x Elle Shanty). I started calling them Toll and Dominator respectively, in the kennel. They were both brindled dogs of decent size, Dominator was the bigger, a real big brute of a dog reminiscent of a coursing type, which of course he wasn't. He'd a massive chest and was extremely long and leggy. Toll was very game and racy looking and looked like he could still compete as he had a very youthful exuberance. Any thoughts that Chris might have paid their passage to Ireland were short-lived. But, I

half-expected it and paid the 120 Euros transport fee and took them home.
Both dogs were very friendly and without nervousness and settled easily into kennel life. I wasted no time in getting them registered for stud duties and started advertising them. I didn't use the Sporting Press which is read by the most people because the Greyhound Weekly, which was a decent paper for the time it ran were offering a full page for a very reasonable price with photographs and colour if wanted. For the same money, the sporting press were offering very little and there was no dealing with them. It was take it or leave it, so I left it. Anyone I knew was buying both weekly papers anyway, so I figured the ads would get enough exposure. The greyhound weekly was run by Malcolm and Julie Sharp in Tipperary and although I never met them in person, they seemed very nice people and genuine greyhound folk.

Bookings were slow, but there were a few enquiries and although slow, the dogs were picking up a bitch here and there. Toll Security looked the best bet. A winner of two group competitions he was picked to run in the TAB TOPGUN invitation at only twenty-one months of age and was the youngest in what many people consider to be the best Topgun line-up ever that included No Intent, Carlisle Jack, Brett Lee, Bright Ebony and Sue Ellen Bale. He ran a great race to finish second and just failed to catch winner No Intent. He missed the break and got pushed wide at the first bend and came from last to almost winning it. It later emerged that Brett Lee had got injured in the race, which might be true as he showed nothing.

Elles Dominator had the misfortune to race predominantly in Tasmania in Oz, which is thought of as being substandard to the city tracks. The standard may not be as high, but plenty of good dogs have come from there. Dominator only had sixteen starts and won eight of them. He broke four records in Tasmania, two track records and two sectional records as I understand it. I spoke to his owner Peter Bohan and he confirmed this. He also told me that the big dog was the fastest born to his prolific mother Elle Shanty who also produced double classic winning Elles Commando amongst a string of top open racers. Her litter to Light Of Fire in addition to Dominator also contained open racers; Elles Flynn (classic finalist and winner of 18 races, including 6 at Wentworth Park) and Elles Amy. Dominator also won at Wentworth park in 30.10 and 30.70. His biggest problem was his trapping ability (which was zero) and the initial twenty yards it took him to get into his stride. I have a video of the dog and his pace once he got going was breath-taking and he simply left good dogs for dead. This litter was so good that it was repeated in 1999 and produced more good dogs including Fired Up Fred winner of the Goulburn maiden classic.

Both dogs were proven from a few mating's they'd had in Australia, before coming to Ireland. Dominator had sired two group winners in Tasmania and Toll had sired Benny's Toll who broke the TR at Wentworth Park in Sydney for the classic 520m distance and was runner-up in the group one Paws of Thunder when strong favourite.

There were two videos made for both Toll and Dominator. Toll's video was a professionally made one that his owner Max Mustapha had made when he decided to let the dog go to Ireland to stand at stud and was well made in a documentary style. It showed all the dog's thirteen wins, his two group race wins and the Topgun final. The two classics he won were the group 2 Vic Peters Memorial classic and the group 3 Dapto puppy classic over 520 and 508m respectively. He broke the second sectional record at Dapto, which as I understand it is from the finish line (first time around) to the end of the back straight.

The video for Dominator was also good and showed some of his wins and also many of the other offspring his dam was famous for. She was a fantastic producer of open class greyhounds.

In 2004, the greyhound-data website wasn't the source of information that it has become and is today. The information on these dogs wasn't there yet and in Ireland at the time, it was all we had to go on in assessing any dog's ability from overseas. I did go onto to the forums and ask Aussies on there about the dogs, but in doing this you do it with a pinch of salt because you'll get a mixed bag of information. You'll get people who have an axe to grind and will rubbish the dogs for one reason or another and you'll get people that will give you an honest answer. You'll also get those who simply don't know but feel the need to comment anyway, rightly or wrongly. You have to separate the wheat from the chaff.

Once I had the dogs it became apparent pretty quickly that Chris didn't own any part of these dogs and he told me that the owners would be getting in touch, which they did shortly after I received the dogs. Peter Bohan who owned and bred Dominator was philosophical. He knew the dog's age was against him (almost seven) and I genuinely don't think he ever expected to get any money from the dog. He was just pleased that the dog would be well looked after and that I was excited to have him. He never asked me for money and I think he understood the stud game better than most. Dominator would be nine years old when his first Irish pups would hit the track and he'd need a big winner or several to have any chance. There hadn't been much interest in the dog in Australia as he was injured early and much of his form was in Tasmania, which isn't respected.

With Toll, it was a different story. His owner Max Mustapha was a nice enough man, but he thought the dog only had to come to Ireland and he'd be inundated with bitches. He'd heard the success stories of Frightful

Flash and Top Honcho and he considered them second rate dogs compared to the stud dogs that were at the top of the tree in Australia. In particular, he couldn't understand the success that Top Honcho had. In his mind, he would never have got bitches in Australia and me telling him that was immaterial didn't wash with him. My point was that the dog *had got* used in Ireland and he'd produced some fantastic dogs and had a great strike rate of open racers. Max considered his dog to be the best Australian Import ever to come to Ireland and to be fair, I think he was right. The dog had won two group races, been second in the biggest race in Australia and won over half of his races. To cap it all, he was already a proven sire and had sired a pup faster than himself in Bennys Toll from his first crop. I think it was Max's dream for a dog to go to Ireland and be a top stud dog and when it became known in Sydney that the dog was going to Ireland, many breeders used him in the weeks before he left. He produced sixteen litters, I believe, before he left for Ireland, so unlike the vast majority of Aussie imports to hit Ireland, there was some demand for him in his home country.

That point is often lost on Irish breeders who fail to realise that there's often a reason why dogs are imported and it's usually that they're not good enough to be wanted at home. Once the dog gets patronage and if it becomes obvious he has the ability as a sire, his race record and anything else doesn't matter. No dog can make it without a certain quantity of bitches and quality amongst them.

Toll Security was sired by Rapid Journey (Amerigo Man x Miss Courtney). Rapid Journey or RJ, was one of the best Australian greyhounds ever if not *the* best, winning eleven group finals and over half a million dollars in prize money. The dog was a freak but wasn't bred from a prolific dam line or deemed fashionably bred. He could lead all the way or come from last to first when he needed to and nearly took the paint off the rails, his track-craft was amazing. He broke the TR at Wentworth park for 520m, then a few years later his grandson Benny's Toll would do the same. RJ was considered by many Aussies to have been a disappointment as a stud dog, but I don't think this is accurate as he did sire plenty of decent stock. Any dog that's a superstar as he was, people expect every pup he throws to be able to run and it doesn't work that way. The same thing happened to the great Ballyregan Bob.

I've heard that RJ was bred from two kennel mates and his dam wasn't much of a racer and didn't produce much else of note other than RJ. If this is true, so what? Stapler's Joe was bred in a similar vein and was a great racer and sire.

Ironically, RJ spent a year in Ireland during the time Toll was here. I don't know how many bitches he got but would surely have got some that might have gone to his son. This didn't help Toll Security at all. I remember at the time there were posts on the forums from Australians saying that he had gone to Ireland as he wasn't wanted anymore in Oz. I don't believe that for a minute. There's begrudgery everywhere it seems!

Toll Security's dam was Sunset Savanah who was a decent city class staying bitch. She did produce some other decent offspring, but nothing else in the class of Toll.

Toll Security didn't get well patronised here, but he got enough to assess his ability as a stud dog. He proved capable of producing outstandingly fast dogs like Bennys Toll, Roxholme Ryan (3 TR's) and a fair few others, but he wasn't as prolific as he might have been. There was an open race bitch called Farantane Sinead who was a maiden bitch when she came and her litter to toll was outstanding. Along with Roxholme Ryan, it also contained Ardbeg Spark, a bitch that won a hot unraced bitch stake at Waterford and was a semi-finalist in the Produce Stakes at Clonmel. She was sold after her unraced stake win for a lot of money. This whole litter raced at a very high standard. I put a couple of good bitches to him myself and there were some top-grade and minor open class runners amongst them, but I expected better to be honest. Tyone Sharon (Arrigle Buddy x Live Commentary) I had particularly high hopes for. She won in Limerick in 28.80 and 28.60 over 525 and won the St.Leger Consolation final over 550 despite not getting the trip. Her early pace won it for her. She had a litter brother Killinan Buddy broke the sprint record at Thurles and her dam Live Commentary was a double classic finalist and prolific brood bitch. Sharon looked a really good bet to produce herself, but although she did throw some fast offspring, there was nothing like herself amongst them. Her litter to Toll were average enough and she had a litter to Dominator that was probably better. She had litters to other dogs too and didn't really produce to any of them.

Dog's like Top Honcho will get a chance in Ireland when they won't in Australia. To be fair to him and Frightful Flash, they had the ability and FF was from an incredible litter, the star of which was his sister Iceni Princess. He also had a litter brother Mightful who may have been better than him too. Michael Dunne imported him too a bit later when it became obvious Frightful Flash was a big hit in Ireland and the dog was almost always booked out. Having two lines of the same blood made sense.

The opposite is also true. Dog's like Farloe Melody, Droopys Sandy and Moral Standards all went to Australia because the demand for them at home wasn't there and they weren't wanted. Before them, went Lively Band, Curryhills Brute and Waverley Supreme (who was probably the most successful of all). But, in the case of these Irish dogs, they were practically all top-class racers, which wasn't the case for the vast majority of early

Aussie imports to hit the emerald isle. So, when the Aussies saw what they considered to be substandard hounds making it at stud in Ireland when many top-class Irish bred racers couldn't make it in Oz, naturally they began to think that their dogs had to be superior. In Max's case, he fully believed this and couldn't understand why his dog wasn't booked out from the moment he arrived. To be fair to him, if either Dominator or Toll had gone to Michael Dunne, the Dunphy's, Michael Daly and one or two others, they would have got many more bitches. As I said earlier, certain areas in Ireland are greyhound hotbeds and if you're not in Munster or within close proximity to it you're at a disadvantage from the start. But, it transcends beyond geographical location too. Many Irish breeders are loyal to certain stud keepers regardless of what dog's they have and will go back to them time after time. That's fair enough. Many people shop religiously at Tesco or Asda for the same reason. But, if you ask them why they only go to Michael Dunne or Dunphy's or whoever it is, you're likely to get an answer like "I've always been lucky there" or "It's handy for me" or similar. There's also the sheep mentality of those who flock to the same stud kennel simply because they know of others that do the same. I think, if one of the top stud kennels heavily marketed a Labrador as the best outcross ever to hit Ireland, he'd get bitches. No, I'm joking here, but I'm sure you get my drift. Rarely in Ireland is the choice of stud dog governed by rational thinking and logic.

I'm not the only stud keeper that struggled. Martin Tucker is based in Roscommon, near Longford and has always had decent stud dogs and I know he's had the same problems and he's been in the game a long time. Kieran Kerley in Monaghan would later have the same trouble with other decent dogs too that included the excellent American import, Flying Stanley.

To be honest, I thought the two dogs would have generated more initial interest than they did. One local breeder Davy McKenna who is one of the few that I have the utmost respect for, he used both dogs twice and did pretty well from them. Davy breeds many litters per year from his dam lines that he's built up over generations. Interestingly, many of his lines go back to the first stud dog we had, Northline, as he used that dog to good effect also.

I started accumulating brood bitches to put to the two dogs. As far as I was concerned, they were as worthy as anything else in the market and deserved to be used and if breeders were going to largely ignore them, I at least would give them a chance.

A few months after the dogs had arrived, they'd only had a handful of matings each and some of these were to my own bitches. I'd set Toll Security at 300 and Elles Dominator at 250, which I believed were excellent value for both. I didn't advertise the price but invited breeders to ask for the free DVD. What I didn't bank on was the number of time wasters that would request the DVD that you'd never hear from again.

A fella I used to discuss bloodlines with on the forums, but hadn't met in person took an interest in the two dogs. His name was Kieran Boles and he had a restaurant business in Dublin and owned a few dogs. His business provided a home delivery service and menus for the top restaurants in the city who didn't do takeaway food. His idea worked in the city, where office workers and other professionals utilised his service.

Many of the top law firms in the city centre when working late would order expensive steaks and charge them to their clients as an expense and eat them at their desks.
Anyway, Kieran was very good at marketing and he came up with a plan to get the two dogs more bitches. I'd already got the video of Toll put onto DVD and Kieran got the details of the top one hundred breeders in Ireland. Next, we designed a voucher that gave the breeder money off, but it was clever as he put the price of the dog's up so it looked as if the voucher was really useful. Toll Security's price was put at 800 and the voucher was for 500 Euro discount off that price, so the breeder would pay 300. Dominators price was put at 750 with the discount giving 500 off, leaving the stud fee at 250. Unfortunately, his race video wasn't of sufficient quality to transfer onto DVD, but we put a photo advert in with his voucher and it looked good.
We thought Toll had the best chance of making it due to his younger age and race record and got a label printed to stick onto the DVD cover that gave it a professional look. We sent the vouchers for the two dogs along with the DVD and the paper advert for

both dogs to those one hundred breeders telling them that they were chosen for their past breeding successes.

Kieran reasoned that this would not only create business for both dogs but would also get some decent quality among them that had already produced open class offspring, which is crucial. He clearly understood the mentality of Irish breeders and he was right to a certain extent.

The dogs did get more bitches. I reckon Toll got about twenty from this campaign (over approximately a year) and Dominator about half that, but it cost money, of course, to get the printing done, the DVD's made, stationery and postage costs. Besides, the newspaper adverts were stepped up and for quite a while I ran a full-page ad every week in the Greyhound Weekly and also plugged the dogs on the forums at every opportunity and advertised them there too. I put up posters for the dogs at the local tracks and can honestly say I did as much to promote the two dogs as I possibly could do. These were still low numbers compared to popular dogs in the leading stud kennels that were getting 50-100 mating's per year, but it was something and it did get business that would definitely have gone elsewhere. It also got a few bitches of quality.

Toll's owner Max would regularly phone me to see how the dog was doing and couldn't understand why the dog wasn't making pots of money for him. To be fair, Chris had sold him a story in Australia that created the myth that Ireland was a goldmine for a dog like his and I think he wondered whether or not he was getting the full picture. I can't blame him as he'd sent the dog over in good faith and expected a return that wasn't forthcoming. I told him about the marketing campaign and as soon as he heard the dog was getting a few bitches from it, he wanted the money. I told him I'd send him money if he wanted, but would have to cut back on the advertising if that was the case as it had to come from the stud fees. He wasn't too pleased to hear this and I wasn't too happy either in that as soon as there was a return from the marketing effort, he wanted all of it, without what I considered due consideration for the outlay that created the extra patronage. I wanted to use the money for advertising and another round of vouchers down the road. I pointed out to him that apart from using the dog a couple of times myself, I hadn't made any money either and was doing all the work. To his credit, he listened and agreed to wait a while and see how things panned out.

From the moment the dogs arrived, I began to hear from Chris less and less. As already stated, he agreed to pay for the adverts in the paper that were left to me to design, which was fine by me. Julie Sharp who edited the paper knew from the start that Chris was to get the invoices, but after a few weeks, she phoned me to say she hadn't got any money and couldn't run the ads without payment. I told her that any ads from this point forward, I would pay for and she agreed to this. She talked about taking action against him for the money, but I don't know how this panned out.

I told him at the beginning that there would be a charge for the dog's keep. This was a safeguard for me to ensure I got something for caring for the dogs if they didn't get bookings. They were with me a good while before the marketing campaign moved them from the red into the black, albeit temporarily. Chris was a strange fella. He sent the dogs to me, hardly knowing me from Adam, yet trusting that I would do right by them. I don't know but always wondered how many other people he'd asked to take the dogs before me. Initially, he checked in with me to see how the dogs were doing but seemed to accept that things were very slow as regards bookings and once he knew the state of affairs never looked for any money or return on whatever it cost him to bring the dogs over from Oz and whatever other costs were associated with all of that. Perhaps he didn't look for it as he realised it wasn't there, but he seemed to be unconcerned. What was also peculiar was the fact that he didn't seem to have any greyhounds of his own and never used the dogs himself or on his behalf. He turned up at the kennels once a few months after the dogs had arrived and I showed him around and showed the two dogs to him, but he didn't seem too interested. He came up to the house, had a coffee and a chat and left me some money for the dogs keep. I only heard from him again once or twice afterwards, before his number became unobtainable and he stopped phoning me. As I said, the whole experience was bizarre. He always seemed a very nice fella if a bit distant or preoccupied and we never shared a cross word.

When a new stud dog starts getting bitches you're on the crest of a wave. The first crop of runners will determine whether or not he makes it and if there is to be a second and third crop. So, any dog must get as many pups on the ground as possible to give him the best possible chance. From my own experience, I reckon you will own twenty greyhounds, on average, to get a really decent one. By that reckoning, an average stud dog will need four hundred pups to produce twenty decent dogs (at a ratio of 20:1). That's why it's so difficult to get a young dog going. Even the busiest young sire will only be busy for maybe eighteen months maximum before matings slow down as breeders wait to see what the early pups are like. If he's deemed a success, he's assured of another eighteen months minimum and he'll receive many more bitches that are proven and of higher quality. I got great experience with these two sires and learnt an awful lot about breeding through this. I was already a good judge of when my bitches were ready for mating, but not all bitches are the same. Generally speaking, the heat season for greyhound bitches lasts up to twenty-one days. The bitch will stand or receive the dog for usually four of those days and this often falls between days ten through to fourteen, with the thirteenth and fourteenth days typically being optimal. But, there are many variations on this. Racefield Kate, one of my broods needed to be mated no later than the twelfth day. Greenpark Betty was another who was mated on the eighteenth day one time but usually was ready by day thirteen. I boarded the majority of the bitches that came as is the norm in Ireland. Most breeders expect you to board their bitches to get two matings done when you're doing natural mating's and two mating's usually ensured there was a litter. I didn't do blood tests or progesterone testing as the dogs were never busy enough to warrant it. I knew the dogs were fertile and when they gave two mating's to a bitch, there were very few misses.

The odd time you'd get a bitch that couldn't be mated as she wasn't right. When this happened, I just told the owner that and there was no harm done.

Both dogs were very good workers that knew what to do and were easy to handle. Toll, in particular, would only show a lot of interest when the bitch was right for mating, or very close to it, so it was useful when a bitch first came in as I learnt to gauge their state of readiness from watching him. Dominator, on the other hand, would be keen a couple of days earlier. He didn't mind whether they were at the optimal time or not!

Both dogs had ability as stud dogs. Hindsight is always perfect and with this benefit, I believe that Elles Dominator was the better stud dog of the two, but I mistakenly placed more faith in Toll Security as his racing career was better on paper. Toll Security's pups also were easier to sell than Dominator's, so I put the better bitches I had to him. Elles Dominator proved to be a decent sire of genuine progeny for all distances. I remember a pup of his I bred that was sold to an Englishman named Des Badger. The pup broke his tail at about seven weeks of age and this necessitated him having to get half of it cut off. I reckoned I'd have to keep this pup, but Des came one day, saw him, wanted him and bought him. The pup went to

Sheffield/Owlerton when reared and schooled by me and eventually became track champion and was a solid A1 dog who never really got injured and won many races for his delighted owner. Dominator had very few runners really in Ireland worth talking about and did very well from the opportunity he got. His sister Elles Amy also produced excellent offspring in the UK. His pups seemed to be pretty tough, like himself.

Not all stud dogs are equal

Once upon a time, I believed that the stud dog played a small role in the ability of his offspring. I believed the bitch contributed 90% to the prowess of any litter. To me, this belief explained why any of the top ten stud dogs produced every grade of dog from the lowest grade to classic winners. Added to this was those few, but highly publicised wonder broods that produced well to every stud dog they went to. I also believed that it was a numbers game pure and simple, meaning that the more bitches a dog got, the more of everything was the outcome, good and bad, fast and slow.

I believe now that the margin between sire and brood is not so clearly defined. The bitch I feel still contributes the most to the genetic make-up of any litter, but the stud dog can make a difference. No question about it. What changed my mind? My own experiences of breeding litters and handling the stud dogs and waiting for their offspring to run shaped how I think nowadays. The greyhound-data site has also played a part. I noticed early on that the statistics that they provide on the site are very useful to breeders. You can see the number of runners any sire has and most importantly you can see the percentage of top performers according to their grading scale. Their grading scale for some runners isn't perfect, but it's good enough. These stats often make interesting reading. I believe any stud dog that has a percentage of 10% or higher top performers is better than average ability, provided he has enough pups running to be able to assess him. If he only has runners from four litters and one litter accounts for 90% of his result, it's not accurate. But, any dog with at least pups from ten litters running or fifty pups plus (that have reached two years old) I feel can be accurately assessed. Top Honcho for example as a super sire has a percentage of 22%. Headbound has a percentage of 18%. Thorgil Tex, an import that got plenty of opportunities, only had a percentage of 8%, as did Toll Security despite both dogs producing some very fast dogs within those stats. Elles Dominator percentage of top runners is 12% and although he didn't get a great chance at stud, he still showed ability, despite getting very few bitches of quality. There are variables within any statistics. The more popular sires will have had higher calibre broods and this will boost their scores, but I think anything showing 12% on this rating is well above average and a good bet indeed.

The leading stud kennels have a big advantage, in that the overflow of bitches for a sire that's booked out can be pushed onto another stud dog and often one that they desperately need bitches for, although this is becoming increasingly less so as AI and frozen implant matings have become more popular. Quite often a bitch isn't ready on the day she's booked in for, so she's already there and needs mating. The breeder's hands are tied to a certain extent. He can leave the bitch there and mate her to a dog he didn't want or he can take her away and try to get another top dog at zero notice. Sometimes this genuinely happens, sometimes it's a deliberate ploy, although it was more common when natural matings were all that available. Nowadays, artificial insemination (AI) with fresh semen is very common, and there's no excuse when this is the procedure as each draw of semen can be used several times. Surgical implants are practised quite often too with the more expensive foreign-based sires, although I'm not in favour of unnecessary surgery. If you want a dog like Brett Lee, for example, you've no choice but to go down this road. I only used a surgical implant once with the dog Like a Shot and got a small litter of weedy pups that weren't much use. Maybe they wouldn't have been any better from a natural mating either, I don't know. But I don't see anything wrong with nature. For the most part, nature and natural matings work just fine. Any surgery carries risks and unless there's no other way than a surgical implant, I wouldn't do it again. With natural mating, the bitch is getting the full ejaculate from the dog. For surgical implants, this is split into maybe ten straws and can be sold as often, which is good business for anyone selling them, but against nature, I feel and the cost of the surgery adds an additional 250 or 300 onto the overall cost. On the positive side, this method allows using a stud dog that's on the other side of the world and enough straws can enable a dog to live on for some time after he's deceased. These are the only advantages to it. If the bitch misses and you go again, you've to pay the vet's bill again.

Any dog starting needs enough bitches if he's to make it. He also needs a percentage of proven ones or at least ones that were open class themselves with the potential to be good producers. As I said earlier, the standard of many of the early imported sires to Ireland left a lot to be desired as regards their ability on the track and they were bought cheaply because they had no future as a stud dog in their own country. In this day and age, no dog can make it on a handful of bitches.

Of course, if a dog proves his worth as a stud dog with good stock and fast offspring, his racing record goes out the window. I remember being unimpressed with Royal Impact when he was first launched in Ireland. His times were pretty ordinary and he was a short course runner by Australian standards, who tend to think of staying ability as strength and lack of as a weakness. Many Irish breeders, by contrast, tend to see staying dogs as one-paced or as plodders, compared to middle distance dogs anyway. Royal Impact was reasonably well used here despite not beginning his stud career in one of the top stud kennels and proved to be an excellent sire, probably as good as any in Ireland during his time. He wouldn't have gotten the same chance down under, which is immaterial now.

Another one is Hondo Black who I remember being similarly unimpressed with. He was an American dog that ran his entire career at one track and whilst he won a local Derby at that track (Southland), I think it's fair to say there were many better dogs in the U.S. than him. Again, he was well used and actually became an excellent sire and unusually for most American imports, actually had a high percentage of early-paced offspring. He was the best American stud dog to come here since the legendary Sandman arrived in the late 1970s.

Michael Dunne

I remember saying on the forums that I wasn't impressed with HB and wouldn't be using him. I didn't slag the dog off, just said that I wasn't impressed with his race record. I got a phone call a few days later from his stud-keeper Michael Dunne who was very annoyed that I had said anything. I told him it was a public forum and I could say what I liked, as could he or anyone else. He made some idle threat, I can't remember the exact words now, to which I just laughed and invited him to come and see me and he hung up. A little while after this, I got another call from his brother who was a lot more polite, although he did let me know early in the conversation that he was a Solicitor, whether he did that as a subliminal threat or for the effect, I'm not sure. He didn't threaten me, but rather reasoned with me that talking down any dog wasn't doing anybody any good. I agreed with him and said that I was only discussing greyhound matters on the forums and didn't mean the dog any harm or intend to annoy anybody. I also added that his brother didn't comment on the forums ever and I wasn't aware that he was on there or following them. I also said that I didn't think it mattered what I said, it wouldn't make or break the dog. He was nice enough, but at the same time, I feel he was warning me off without being blunt about it. I said I didn't appreciate being threatened by his brother and that was the end of it.

To be fair to Michael Dunne, he has made a huge contribution to Irish greyhound breeding and he started the Australian-dog-mania that became prevalent in Ireland from the mid-'90s and continues to the present day. He brought quality dogs in and marketed them skillfully. He cultivated a strong relationship with many of Ireland's breeders and that's what it's all about to succeed here. In the early days, he had John Fitzpatrick working his stud dogs when it was all-natural matings and this association would have been popular with many Irish breeders who would have been familiar with Fitzpatrick through Sandman and other dogs he handled. The Aussie invasion started with Frightful Flash and continued through Top Honcho, Dave's Mentor and many others. Not every dog he's imported has had the same level of success, which is only to be expected and not every dog he's brought in has made it. What he does ensure is that every dog he has will get a chance. Dunne also invested in clinical facilities and was one of the first to offer blood and progesterone testing for the visiting bitches. Breeding is far from an exact science and it's only when a dog has had an opportunity to prove his worth that you will know for sure what you have. It's not enough that a dog is fast and a classic winner. These things won't guarantee his success as a sire. Nor will breeding alone or breeding and speed guarantee it. It takes genetic ability and the passing of that to his offspring to guarantee success and no one can predict in advance whether this will happen. The proof is always in the pudding or the pups in this case.

Frightful Flash started it all off as regards Australian blood becoming popular and to be fair, Irish bloodlines are now saturated with it. A pure Irish track-bred greyhound is very hard to find now and in some ways, it's a pity. Irish greyhounds and Irish thoroughbred racehorses used to be considered the finest in the world. I think certain Australian bloodlines have clicked better with Irish bloodlines than others. The Head Honcho sire line has been a revelation and Brett Lee has suited Irish lines very well too. Unfortunately, when breeding greyhounds, it's largely trial and error. You have to breed litters and assess the offspring to deem anything a success or a failure. It takes both time and money as it takes two years to judge a litter.

A couple of year's later, I fancied using Daves Mentor (Head Honcho x Best of Bev) who Dunne had and I always liked the dog. I thought he was an exceptional sire of early and all-round pace and very genuine offspring. He was also from a very good dam line. I phoned to book him and spoke to a girl who took the booking date and said someone would come back to me to confirm. At this time, they were using fresh semen and AI, so there would have been no problem with availability. I booked this as soon as the bitch came in season, so about ten to twelve days before the job needed to be done. The only disadvantage to this type of system is that you have to leave the bitch there for a day or two. This ensures they test her and do the insemination at the right time, but it means that the breeder has two trips, whereas, with a natural mating, he could come and get the service and go home with the bitch immediately afterwards. The girl explained the bitch would have to be left and I agreed, despite the seventy miles each way distance. All that remained was a return call to confirm the appointment.

The call wasn't forthcoming in the week that followed and I assumed there was bad feeling on Dunne's part from the time he'd phoned me over the Hondo Black issue and I booked another dog somewhere else. I think it was the day before I would have travelled that I got a call from Dunne's team asking if I was coming. I explained that as I'd had no contact from them for over a week, I'd made other arrangements and that was that. I could have cancelled the other dog, but I'm the type of person that when I arrange or agree to something, I tend to stick to it. When I used Frightful Flash, I found Michael Dunne to be a bit odd, in that he was there but seemed to avoid acknowledging or speaking to us. If he is the type of person that finds it easier to deal with people over the phone, that's his prerogative and I don't care, but to use the phone to make empty threats to someone that has given him business in the past is bad practice in my view. I saw a funny side to the whole thing and bore him no ill will, hence my trying to book Dave's Mentor later on. It's a funny world!

I believe the stud dog can make as much as 30 - 40% impact on a litter, with the bitch supplying the majority of the genetic input. No stud dog, no matter how good, can make up for a useless bitch.

Trendy Leigh (Gun Law Osti x Sobbing Sal)

Trendy came to me in early 2007. Kieran Kerley from Monaghan was a breeder with a great interest in stud dogs and bloodlines. He was one of the first to use both Toll Security and Elles Dominator. He negotiated the leasing of Brett Lee's litter brother Trendy and asked me to stand the dog at stud as he'd no experience at the time with stud dogs. I was delighted to have the dog. I got a weekly rate for looking after the dog and a small percentage of his stud fee which began at 750 Euros (less 50 luck). Unlike with Toll and Dominator, I couldn't use him myself for free.

He wasn't much to look at and like his brother Brett, only raced at around 65 lbs. When anyone came for mating and saw the other two dogs, they usually remarked how much better they looked.

Trendy wasn't only a litter brother to the great Brett Lee but was a Group Two race winner at Cannington over 530m and a finalist in the group one National Sprint final at the Meadows. He wasn't as fast as his more illustrious brother, but he could certainly run a bit. He was also a proven sire in Oz and had already a decent number of good offspring. He'd mated his share of bitches down under and his connections probably thought he'd gotten what patronage he was going to get on his home turf.

We got a DVD of his race wins copied, including his group win, in which he was impressive looking coming from behind to win and started to market the dog through the usual channels. The dog did start to get a few bitches from the start but was never what you'd call busy. Certainly not as busy as I expected him to be, given that his brother was commanding a 5000-stud fee including surgical implant as he never left Australia. Nor was he ever as busy here as his half-brother Head Bound who never won a single race, yet benefitted from his location in one of the leading kennels and also from the mentality of the average breeder. Now, Head Bound's ability as a stud dog soon became apparent when his pups hit the track and he became a very good sire, as good as Brett Lee in my opinion and considerably cheaper.

The dam Sobbing Sal was a top-class racing bitch and an excellent producer who produced class in every litter. Apart from Head Bound, an earlier litter to Head Honcho also produced Hotshow Ben and Hotshow Sam who did well at stud too for the opportunity given to them. She had a litter to Just The Best that produced the flying Big Daddy Cool and Balintore Brave, the latter ran all his races in Ireland before going to stud. He was decent if not a top-class performer, who like most of the stud dogs from this bitch, performed well at stud. Her offspring like herself were on the small side. The dogs rarely topped sixty-six pounds and many of the bitches were in the low mid-fifties. Very few of the bitches produced anything of note themselves. Even Shotgun Sal litter sister to Trendy and Brett Lee was a poor producer. There were pups advertised from her litter to Token Prince that ended up in Ireland and they cost a small fortune. I remember them being noteworthy for not chasing genuinely.

Trendy too had ability as a sire and really should have attracted a better class of bitch than he did. Few of the bitches he got here were proven or open class themselves. With all the stud dogs available from this Sobbing

Sal line, it's perhaps in some ways understandable he wasn't used more.

He was a funny little dog. Very clean in the kennel and no problem to handle and care for, but sometimes he'd turn his nose up at a bitch for no apparent reason, as she was ready. I sometimes had to bring out Dominator or Toll and pretend that they were going to mate the bitch, then let trendy on at the last minute. This seemed to work well as he'd show more interest when there was another dog on the scene, but it was a quirk he showed occasionally. He did produce some very good greyhounds, however.

One of the bitches he got turned up in very poor condition, with traces of mange. I had a separate kennel block at the time and kept her in there in isolation, in case she contaminated the others. This mating produced Corporate Attack who was, in my mind, the best-staying dog seen in Ireland for many years and the majority of the litter were also very fast. Corporate Attack won the Group 1 Corn Cuchulainn at Harold Cross over 750 and smashed the 850 clock at Shelbourne, taking a massive seventy spots off the old record. The dog won top-class races at all the leading tracks in Ireland in near-record times and his weight fluctuated sometimes three or four pounds between races! Always owner trained, I always wondered what he might have been in other circumstances. He was an extraordinary dog who also was top-class over 550, winning the Group 2 Champion Plate at Shelbourne and the Barry Open 600 there too. He was a big dog and Shelbourne Park was perfect for him.

Even though he was a quarter-finalist in the Irish Derby when his career finished, there was nobody who wanted to use the dog, as he was seen as a stayer and unfashionably bred too. Again, if he had been put with a leading stud-keeper, he might have got a chance. He would have been a good export to Australia too from an all Irish dam line. Interestingly, his dam never won a race but was a decent producer. Again, if a dog can produce substantially better than itself, their own race ability is soon forgotten. He got a few local bitches at stud, but nothing worth talking about. I think, given an opportunity this dog would have been a good stud dog as he was a flying machine and very, very genuine.

After a year or so and Trendy having a number of bitches, Kieran Kerley decided to have a go at standing the dog himself, which he managed to do fine. I think his fee in Ireland peaked at one thousand Euros less luck.

Trendy Leigh wasn't used as much as he might have been. He clearly had the ability as a sire and had also been a decent dog in his own right, not just a litter brother to Brett Lee.

Litter brothers at stud

Breeders have always tried to use litter brothers of top dogs in a bid to replicate success on the cheap. Does it work?

It's hard to say or compare the two because the inferior or less popular brother will not get the same number or quality of bitches. I think if the dog is fast enough himself to warrant going to stud, there's no reason why he shouldn't produce as well as a litter brother. If he wasn't fast himself, I wouldn't bother with him, that's just my take on it. Sometimes, a dog will get badly injured in schooling when showing promise and fail to overcome injury. Head Bound was retired after three winless races. Word was at the time he was doing flying trials, but only his connections know for sure. Tales abound in greyhounds of what might have been, only for injury!

On the reverse side of this, litter sisters to top dogs have and will always be used in breeding and many of them produce quality offspring, regardless of whether or not they were any good themselves. It's in the blood, as they say, sometimes it works and sometimes not. I've always subscribed to this theory.

Finland

In the summer of 2006, I visited Finland and saw their greyhound racing scene. It's run exclusively by hobbyists and the most common scenario is a household will have one or two greyhounds. The dogs live in the home as their winters are so cold and I was amazed at how race dogs adapted so easily to doubling as both pets and race dogs. The dogs were fantastically clean as living in the home will ensure and they were well contented as they were getting far more attention than is the case in a traditional kennel set-up. A lot of Irish would think dogs would get soft from this kind of living, but it seemed to work fine. Dogs are very adaptable animals and greyhounds really do have a lot to offer as pets as well as racers. Just outside Helsinki, they have a track at Tampere that's supposed to have been modelled on Wentworth Park in Sydney and it looked a good galloping circuit.

Changes In The Game.

When I was training dogs in the 1990s, the prize money for a standard race was around fifty quid. In 2004, when I was racing again after a few years out of the game, the prize money for the same type of race had jumped to two hundred quid. Also, the Irish Greyhound Board (IGB) had started to pump money into the sport from around the year 2000 that saw the infrastructure and facilities at the nine tracks they owned upgraded and improved. This included the total switching from grass to sand at every track, the improvement of food and beverage facilities and comfortable furnishings. Greyhound racing was suddenly going upmarket and trying to rid itself of the poor man's racehorse image and the target market was young professionals who would come greyhound racing and have a meal and a few drinks. In short, the IGB was investing to attract a different client than the owner-trainer who made up 95% of the turnstile's takings in prior times.

In theory, this was good news. Most tracks got a face-lift, a decent restaurant and food options and you also got to see the racing on tv from the Dublin tracks if the night coincided with theirs. This meant punters could see and bet on racing from two tracks. Better prize money should have been great news to owners and trainers too. In the major competitions, this was undoubtedly so, but it made a huge difference to the ordinary graded races and not for the better in my view. Getting races for your dogs was never a problem in the pre-investment days. You could get a race almost every week if you wanted at the same track and could race twice in the week at alternating tracks. Everybody wanted the extra prize money on offer, which meant suddenly, it was very difficult to get races due to the demand for them and extra dogs that appeared seemingly overnight looking for races. This is a problem that has not been addressed to the present day and many people have left the sport or sold dogs to England simply because they can't get races for them. I know of plenty of cases where pups had qualified, their cards left with manager's four or five weeks in advance and they allowed the time to run out, meaning the dogs had to be requalified again. This is not good enough. Apart from anything else, dogs need to race to improve. Wonder-dogs aren't that common and most dogs tend to improve naturally through the grades with regular racing. You see this in England all the time where dogs show steady improvement through running week in, week out.

What has become harder again is getting races for dogs that don't get 525 or want the longer distances as outside of Dublin, provincial tracks run mainly 525 and 550. There might only be one or two sprint races on any given night out of a ten-card, and if you want a race longer than six hundred yards, you'll be waiting!

Another factor with these changes was that races became much harder to win with the better prize money. We used to win loads of races in the '90s simply because our dogs were always well-schooled, fit and knew the track well. Races were easily obtained and a lot of people weren't race-ready then. With better money on the table, more trainers became commonplace and the dogs were usually fit and ready.

Trialling also became a nightmare, suddenly there was maybe one hundred dogs in front of you and a long wait.

There has always been decent money available for fast dogs and the prices for top-class dogs has gone up and up.

Unfortunately, the prices for average graders have gone down and continued to do so. In some cases, there is no market anymore for some dogs. Bottom grade dogs might fetch two hundred if you can find a buyer. There used to be a ready market for a 30.00 dog over 525, which is 29.50 today. There's little or no market for these dogs now.

These changes brought more people into the sport. More owner's who needed a trainer, syndicates too that would buy dogs and spread the cost between members, but it has created a glut of dogs that remains to the present day and it's the ordinary working man that keeps a couple of dogs that has been penalised. He can't get races, he tries to get the dog trials around his working week to keep the dog fit, in case he gets a race and the ready selling market that used to be there for graders is largely gone.

People are breeding litters of pups and end up practically giving them away at ridiculously low prices just to offload them. Well-bred pups can be bought today from as little as three hundred euros at twelve weeks of age. The new regulations mean they now have to be microchipped too upon sale, so if you get a vet to do this and vaccinate as well, you're looking at fifty euros per pup on top of your stud fee, rearing costs, litter registration and marking costs. There's a fair bit of work and expense in getting a litter to twelve weeks of age. More needs to be done for the average owner and breeder, but it's been this way for twenty years. Pup prices haven't gone up in at least fifteen years! You'll buy a well-bred greyhound at twelve weeks cheaper than a yorkshire terrier at eight weeks!

The IGB is a semi-state body and they should have made ownership of track greyhounds separate from the Irish Coursing Club (ICC). Many people love racing but are against coursing, yet the fee structure of the ICC is still in place. You have to deal with them in everything from naming a dog to a transfer of ownership, to registering a litter and they do nothing for the money they make. They are very difficult to deal with and exist solely to make money as far as I'm concerned. There's a lot more I could say but genuine owners and breeders know where I'm coming from.

SkillNets 2007

There was a greyhound trainers course launched in 2007. I was one of twelve successful applicants chosen to do this course. It was held in the old Army barracks in the Curragh in Kildare. There was a Fetac Level 5 qualification to accompany it and it was the very first recognised qualification ever to do with greyhound training in Ireland. It was funded by EU money, which must have quickly run out as I don't think there's been any more of these courses ran since.

The course was a week-long and I really enjoyed it. We had classes and discussions during most days and there was a trip to a race track every night that included a meal at the venue and free admission. We visited Newpark Stud (where they demonstrated an AI procedure for us) in Clonmel also Pat Dalton's place in Golden. Both places were enjoyable visits, but I particularly liked Dalton's kennel set up, which replicated that of the American racing tracks. The race dogs had small individual crate type kennels that could stack on top of each other. This saved space and they were very well designed. The brood bitches had individual kennels with a system similar to a cat flap where they could go outside to relieve themselves as needed, then back into the warmth of the bed. This meant that they didn't need to be let out regularly, which takes the most time in any kennel.

There was a lecture by the famous greyhound vet Plunkett Devlin and this was probably the best thing of the entire week. He discussed greyhound injuries and answered every question put to him.

It was a most enjoyable week. Everything was laid on and no expense was spared. We had a mini-bus to take us to different places and all food was of a very good standard. I thought I was going to burst from eating all week and no exercise. I had arranged a local greyhound fella to look after my dogs for the week.

I can't say I learnt an awful lot from the course as I think it was being piloted as an entry-level into greyhound training, but being with like-minded people for a week, talking greyhounds as well as seeing how other set-ups operated was educational and interesting. I got a booking for Toll Security out of it too. If this had become a regular course it would have been great for young people coming into the sport that would give them some paperwork that would hopefully lead to more courses and recognition for the work they do. Above all, it should have paved the way for a career structure in the industry, because unless you get a job with a trainer or work for yourself, there's nothing else out there and no recognition for it. Even working in kennels with a trainer in most cases is just donkey work and you might only be mucking out more than learning anything useful. Again, it was an opportunity that seems to have been shelved, at least for lack of funds.

Good times and bad

From mid-2004, I decided to concentrate full time on the dogs and I left the paint business. My relationship with my Da had only worsened over time and we rarely saw eye to eye on anything. I remember the first mating that Toll Security had and he was helping me with that. The dog was having difficulty entering the bitch and he thought one thing and I thought another. To cut a long story short, an argument ensued and he ended up walking off and leaving me holding both dog and bitch.

Although it didn't seem like it in the immediate aftermath, this was a good thing as I developed a method of holding both dog and bitch together for almost every mating thereafter. I would place a stool handy, nearby where I working and I would kneel and manoeuvre the dogs into place using my left hand for the bitch and my right for controlling the dogs. I would slide my left arm in under the bitch just in front of her hind legs and grip the outside of the hind leg furthest away from me, where I could not only hold her firm but also lift her upward if necessary. My right arm and hand would guide the dog and my hand would grip his rump where I could manoeuvre and adjust him into striking position. It was one of the few times when having massive hands was an advantage! There was a couple of times that I had to tie a bitch's lead to something, but I got very adept at handling the two dogs together that even when I had an owner on hand to hold the bitch, I preferred it the other way. I remember applying for a trainer's licence in 2007 (I think) and the control steward from Longford called in to see the kennels (Pat? His surname escapes me now) and I was in the middle of a mating when he walked in. He was amazed that I was managing the two dogs just fine on my own.

I was making enough money to live on with the dogs I was rearing and from puppy sales, where I often got to rear them on as well afterwards. Having the use of the two stud dogs meant I wasn't paying for stud fees. I had no shortage of English and Irish people wanting dogs reared and I increased my paddock space to accommodate more. I would have been happy enough just to breed and rear pups and push the stud dogs, but to make a living in Ireland it's not enough. You need to do schooling and often train as well. I was charging twenty-five euros per pup, per week for rearing. If they needed schooling, this went up to forty euros per week. Training racing dogs at the time paid fifty euros a week, so training was much more lucrative when you had a few to train as the food costs to feed both types would be roughly the same. A growing sapling will eat about twice what a race dog will eat in quantity, but the quality of the racing dog's grub would be better.

The biggest and most crippling thing in any business is overheads and I quickly realised that I had to cut costs to the bone or I wouldn't last or make a living. I did my own worming and used mostly Panacur wormer that I bought by the litre. I believe this is the best wormer out there and it's suitable for all dogs of any age. I think at the time it was about sixty euros per litre and it would dose a lot of dogs. Young pups, especially up to three months, need a lot of worming, every two weeks. Once they get to three months, you can do them every month to six months and then twice monthly after that. I believe this is what worked best for me. Now and again I'd use a different wormer just for a change.

I also did my own puppy vaccinations and bought the seven-in-one vaccination for seven or eight euros each from a 'friendly' chemist. The vets were successful in making this prescription medicine, so you needed a friendly chemist to sell them to you as most wouldn't.

I got a 28% protein greyhound complete feed at a reasonable price that I ordered by the pallet and paid for cash on delivery to ensure I got it at the best price. I used this as the mainstay of the pups' diet and I would supplement this with fresh tripe and eggs that I got for nothing. The eggs would have had a best before date of a few days previous, but they were always fresh. Tripe is a great food for growing pups as it has a high-fat content and they enjoy it. It was cow tripe and the only thing was that I had to cut it and handle it, but it was free food and good stuff at that. I used to give the pups 'lamlac' as well or any other substitute lamb or cow powdered milk. The pups love these powdered kinds of milk, but you have to get the dosage right as too rich will scour the pups as I quickly found out. When I had no tripe, I'd give the pups some raw beef that I used to get from the kennels of the meath hunt outside Kells.

The dogs that I took to train and the pups for schooling got a racers diet that consisted of the same dry meal, but with an egg and a pound to a pound and a half of beef per dog, depending on size.

Dry dog meals are marketed as complete foods and many rearers and trainers will feed these and nothing else. It would have been easier and cheaper for me just to use meal and nothing else, but when you see how much happier a dog is to get a bit of meat, it tells its own story.

I used flea collars for the race dogs, stud dogs and my brood bitches and sprayed the paddock reared pups with a solution called Malathion liquid mixed with water. This was a product that was used for keeping insects off roses and another greyhound man told me about it. It was good stuff. If you put it on a dog that had fleas you'd see them leaving immediately and it was fine for the dogs' coats. Later on, it became unavailable and I switched to using thirty drops of tea tree oil in a litre of water that I'd put into a spray bottle and spray the dogs regularly with it.

I used good barley straw when I could get it and paper straw when I couldn't. It's sometimes difficult to get decent straw that holds together for a while, but dogs prefer it to anything else.

I've always been a big believer in exercise and that a well-exercised dog is a happy one. I always kept the stud dogs within three or four pounds of what they'd have raced at and I used to let them gallop now and again. I reasoned that not only was it good for them, but having them reasonably fit was only common sense. My broods I would keep in a similar condition when not in pup. As I've said earlier, any pups I reared were in decent sized paddocks and they got out of the paddocks at least once per day (usually twice) where they'd always use themselves, which wasn't always the case in the paddocks. Pups get complacent even in the biggest of paddocks and if they never get out of them, it's not good for their development. They need to not only run long straights but to chase and twist and turn regularly. The best aspects of paddock rearing are when you have a number of them running parallel to each other, pups will run up and down the fences racing each other, and the safety that the paddock brings. Looking back, it would have been a lot easier on myself if I didn't spend the time I did on this exercising and ensuring the dogs got out for free running and no-one would have known any different. But, I believed in what I was doing and was hoping to create something really special. It was important to me that the dogs were as content as could be and I got a certain satisfaction in knowing that I was doing all I could in providing this. There are risks in giving pups freedom and some will injure themselves, but that's part and parcel of the game. What use will they be if they've never had the opportunity to really extend themselves?

Accidents will happen when working with dogs. One day Toll and Dominator got out of the paddock. One of the dogs had made a hole in the fence and they got out through it. I was feeding pups a couple of acres away when I caught sight of them in the open pasture. Unfortunately, the nearest neighbour to me, whose property bordered mine on one side, was out in the garden with the dog barking and they made a beeline in that direction when they heard the noise. By the time I got there, probably three minutes later, the dog was dead and his intestines were hanging out and the two stud dogs were standing over him. I don't know if it was one or both of them that did the damage, but that's the danger with greyhounds. They are so prone to chasing any small animal that moves and most of them will kill whatever they catch. They're primarily dogs that are bred to hunt by sight and when they lift something at speed it invariably results in death, whether intended or not.

Things were good. I had litters on the ground, pups to rear and I was making it pay. Greyhound data was a big help in this. Not only was I networking and creating business through participation on the forums, but I could advertise my pups for free with multiple pictures. It was a game-changer as far as promoting a kennel was concerned. If I could have made enough money from rearing, breeding and schooling pups alone, it would have been perfect, but I had to go racing as well. I had to take on a few race dogs for people as well as race my pups to sell them on. When you're racing on top of everything else, it really makes a huge demand on your time. My workday started at about seven in the morning. My rearing and schooling work would be finished by six in the evening. If racing that night, dogs have to be kennelled by seven-thirty. You could be then waiting two hours or more for your race, then home again. I often didn't get back to the kennels until eleven at night and the dog would have to be fed and I usually would let the other adult dogs out into the paddock to empty before I went home, which was another forty minutes away. Winning a race is a great feeling, but for me I was always happiest working with the pups, exercising them over the fields and watching them develop. I grew to enjoy the breeding side of it as well as I always had a big interest in bloodlines. I grew to hate having to go to the tracks on race nights, especially when you were there that morning, maybe trialling pups. At the height of it, I had about eighty dogs made up of the stud dogs, brood bitches, race dogs and pups of various ages. I was working about eighty hours per week and to no great surprise, my back started giving me problems.

Many Irish people keep a couple of dogs as a hobby and dream one day of being able to give up their jobs and work with greyhounds' full time. Some try it. Most that do, fail. I did it for several years and for the most part, I enjoyed it and I made it pay (if you're interested in more details of costs etc than I've given here, I wrote an eBook in 2005 that was available on Greyhound-data for some time, I have included it here at the end of the book). It supported me and my family, and I met a lot of decent people along the way. I was lucky in the sense that I had kennels to start with and didn't have to pay rent or buy a place. I also had a van that was my own. As previously outlined, I obtained the use of two stud dog's services for free anytime I wanted. In time, I was able to afford to build more kennels and do a make-over on the existing ones. I also extended my range of paddocks with professional fencing and puppy houses made of shiplap timber. I learnt an awful lot during this time. The man who keeps a couple of greyhounds and trains them in his spare time has a big advantage over anyone handling a large number of dogs. The biggest advantage is time. The more dogs you're working the less time you have for each one. There are only so many hours in the day and you must prioritise your time and the jobs that have to be done. My routine would be to paddock the adult dogs in rotation to let them empty, whilst I did whatever mucking out needed doing. I used sawdust on the floors, which was good, so if a dog peed it would soak it up, stop it running and mask the odour. It meant that you could lift the soiled area and reapply with fresh stuff where necessary. Once a week, I brushed all the floors out, disinfected the areas with Jeyes fluid and spread fresh sawdust down when all was dry. I'd feed all the dogs then. I generally fed adult dogs once per day. If a dog was racing that night he'd get an egg with honey and glucose about ten in the morning and his dinner after racing. The pups in the paddocks would all be fed and their water topped up. Once all were fed, the exercise would start and if I was trialling that day, I'd start to prepare for that. If I wasn't trialling, I'd groom the race dogs and tend to any medication or worming that needed doing. The brood bitches were checked for coming in season every day and if in pup, were given whatever they needed as regards worming and extra food etc. Most dogs that would be racing that night were kept on the lead just long enough to empty. In the afternoon, the feeding would begin for all the dogs and the monotony of letting the dog in and out of paddocks or the open field would continue until I either went racing or home for the night. At the height of the operation, daily feeding and mucking out alone took about four hours. In between the daily necessities of kennel life, time would be made for the odd mating and sometimes people would come to view and/or buy pups. There was a four-hundred-yard sand gallop facility that opened outside Slane and it was very good. It had a lure on it and it opened at the end to ensure the dogs could pull up safely and with plenty of room. It was only thirty euros a month for as many runs as you wanted and was open every day. I used this for racers and pups starting off. It was particularly good for the latter as there was no one around to distract or put the pups off, which sometimes can happen at the licensed tracks. I sometimes brought owners here to watch their dogs and to assist in hand-slipping them with me. In most cases, if they chased the lure up this gallop, they'd take to it at the track as well. The odd one though would run the straight gallop fine and baulk and stop chasing on the track.

I had some very decent owners. There was a couple in London that bought two pups from me at twelve weeks and left them with me to rear on. They visited a couple of times to see the pup and took a real interest in seeing the pups grow and develop. Their pups were nearly reared at the time when I noticed the dog pup holding his leg at a funny angle one morning. I took him out of the paddock and could see the leg was broken at the elbow joint. The couple were due at the kennels later that day. All I could do was show them the dog, who wasn't showing signs of pain. I got a vet to look at the leg and he advised putting the dog to sleep. I had some twelve-week-old pups in the place by Toll Security out of a bitch called Funtime Fliss. I offered them one free of charge as although I was under no obligation to offer anything, I felt for the people as they were decent and I saw how disappointed they were earlier over the broken leg. They accepted the offer and although I gave the pup away, they paid me to rear it. The bitch was named Funtime Jag and despite being no world-beater, she won eight races for them and they really enjoyed going to see her run. In England, this type of ownership is still possible as races are plentiful, dogs are attached to the track and are paid appearance money to run every week. This gives the owners the chance to see them regularly and for the dogs themselves to improve through regular racing. The bitch won three in a row and one point, going up a grade each time. It didn't matter to the couple that she wasn't top-class, they just loved to see her run, win or lose.

The downside of rearing or training dogs in Ireland is you're almost always a month in arrears of payment. Most people pay no problem, but there's always some that don't or do their best to avoid paying. I was lucky or maybe chose carefully most of the time who I would take on as an owner, but I was about to make a mistake in judgement that would cost me not only a lot of money, but it also led to a foundation that sickened me to the point where I grew very disillusioned with the game.

There was a working-class fella from Essex who had very limited involvement in greyhounds. He frequented the local track at

Romford and thought he knew a lot more than he did. Somehow, he had the notion of going to Australia and buying a dog good enough to run in the Irish Derby before going to stud. We all have hopes and dreams, but this was a particularly ambitious one by anyone's standards. For one thing, Aussie dogs chase an inside hare that's quite different than what they chase here. Nevertheless, he ended up buying remarkably well. He bought a dog, who was considered a decent open race dog, but would never be expected to win a major race.

I believe he bought the dog for the equivalent of ten thousand Australian dollars. The dog's dam was an open-class bitch and litter sister to the infamous Split The Bill who was notorious for throwing many fighters, as well as dogs with serious speed. This is also the same dam-line as Brett Lee's dam. The dog had won a heat of the Adelaide Cup at Angle Park but wasn't fancied in the final that contained the hot favourite Carlisle Jack and also the talented Henerik Bale. It was suggested to the new owner that he let the dog run in the final anyway, which he did. To the surprise of many, he won the final and the prize money of fifty thousand dollars. How's that for luck?

The dog's name was Brookside Bear. He raced another few times in Oz without a win, before he was shipped over to the UK and then Ireland. The dog went to Seamus Graham to be got ready for the Irish Derby and was going very well (according to the owner) before he broke his hock. He was then put with Michael Daly to stand at stud. He turned out to be a decent sire from very limited opportunities. He also had a stint in the UK at stud. Australian's would have had no interest in the dog at stud. He wasn't what they considered a top-drawer runner and his sire-line although very fast, wasn't deemed fashionable. His sire was a sprinter type called Applaud and he wasn't popular either down under.

Anyway, the owner contacted me in early 2004 and asked me to do some work for him. He'd bought a brood bitch that was a litter sister to Scottish Derby winner Micks Mystic and wanted to put her to his dog when she came in season.

I picked this bitch up from a place about twenty miles away from my kennels. I rang the day beforehand and told the fella not to feed her the following morning so there'd be less chance of her getting sick or worse. He must have fed her about twenty minutes before I arrived as she threw up a dishful of undigested dog meal in the back of the van. Anyway, she was a big strong black bitch of about seventy-four pounds and settled in well. He had another bitch that he sent to me called Maid In Adelaide who was by Head Honcho out of a daughter of True Temptation who was the dam of Token Prince and a string of top performers. As she was closely related to his stud dog, he agreed to breed her to Dominator and I whelped her down and reared and sold the pups for him, which were quite easily sold. This bitch was only a grader but won races in both Oz and the UK. When the black bitch was ready, I took her down to Michael Daly to be mated and when she pupped, I whelped her down too and reared the pups. Initially, he planned to sell the majority of the pups off at twelve weeks of age and he probably needed to as his kennel bill was growing all the time. I wrote out an ad for the pups and it was put in the paper along with the internet. Only one of the pups sold from within Ireland. Another one went to an owner in England but the rest stayed with me for rearing.

The bill was rising all the time. Initially, he would pay regularly enough, but then he got two months behind before he'd pay for one month. If this had continued just a month behind, I wouldn't have minded, but his payments became more and more erratic. He came over twice to see his pups and the second time he tried to be clever about it by not telling me he was coming. I was at Dundalk trialling this morning when he phoned me saying he was at the kennels. I said: "Well I'm in Dundalk and won't be back for two hours". I wasn't too pleased that he'd just arrived and couldn't see the point of why someone would do that, unannounced. Did he not trust me or something? Anyway, he was there when I arrived back and I showed him his dogs and he came out over the fields with his saplings for a gallop. He was staying in Kells town and asked if I'd meet him that night for a drink. I'd no desire to do so but thought he probably wanted to give me some money as at this point his bill was around two grand. So, I didn't go home that evening and met up with him for a couple of drinks. In the end, I had to ask him straight out: "Have you any money for me?" He said he hadn't had a chance to get to the bank and would send it over the following week. I knew now that I had a problem as it was some time from when he'd paid me and when he would come over bold as brass without money, it was very unlikely he'd send it on. I was very annoyed and told him I couldn't feed his dogs for nothing. He was all apologies and gave the usual bullshit lines. I left and went home.

I got one small payment, I think about three hundred from him a couple of weeks later and nothing after that. His six pups were big brutes, all over seventy-five pounds weight and were coming up to a year old. The one that I was rearing for a UK owner was collected at a year old. I was ringing him every week at this stage and things were getting heated. He said to give him a couple of weeks as he was talking to people in the UK that wanted to buy some of them and as soon as that was done, I'd be squared up. Needless to say, this never came to pass. When he was over in Ireland that time, he let it slip that he had dogs in Waterford as well, that someone was doing for him. This made sense in some ways. I realised that the months he wasn't paying me, he was paying the guy in Waterford and vice-versa. So, eventually, he rang me one day and said that he wanted to keep all his dogs in the one place and that place was Waterford. I said that's fine and welcomed the news. He said a transporter would collect them the following day. "They can go as soon as the bill is paid", I said. "I'll get you fixed up in the next week or so," he said, meaning after the pups had gone. I said: "No way, they have to be paid for first". I then saw a side to him that was new to me. He went ballistic on the phone threatening this and that and I hung up the phone.

The following week, I was qualifying pups at Mullingar one morning and exchanged social pleasantries with the control steward Tony Fahy. The job done, I returned to the kennels and was just back ten minutes when Tony Fahy's jeep pulled into the yard. I was surprised, to say the least, as I'd just been talking to him and he wasn't due to call for ear-marking or anything like that. He announced that the ICC had received a complaint and that he had to check that your man's dogs were there. Apparently, after our phone conversation, he'd phoned the ICC and told them basically I'd kidnapped his dogs and probably sold them. There was no chance of me selling them as the papers were in his name and he had them. How could I sell them? I certainly wasn't foolish enough to try.

"Why didn't you tell me about this in Mullingar?" I asked him.

"I couldn't" he answered, meaning forewarned is forearmed and if he was sly about it, there was less chance I would move the dogs or something else equally ridiculous.

One thing that could have been harmful to me was that he had all the earmarks of the relevant dogs including the one that had gone to the UK the week before. I told him one of them went to England and luckily enough I phoned the fella and he confirmed that was the case, or I'd have been liable for that pup I suppose. I pointed to the paddock where the pups were and said: "Away you go then". It was a rainy time and you can imagine the warm welcome he got from five extremely friendly saplings, each one trying to lick his face. So, in he went and checked their earmarks and emerged shortly afterwards, mucked up to the eyeballs.

"So, what happens now," I asked him, knowing nothing would happen once he could ascertain all dogs were accounted for. I just wanted to see what he'd say. He mumbled something about reporting back that all dogs were accounted for. I told him that the ICC got a good income from me each year through all the relevant fees I had to pay (mating certs, ear-marking, puppy registrations, litter registrations etc) and he's here because some Englishman that couldn't pay his bill had made a complaint over the phone and a false one at that. Fahy said very little and knowing how the ICC operates, I wasn't surprised. Anything that might hurt them in the pocket or publicly has to be investigated and in the slyest way possible. I can understand to a certain extent that he was doing as he was told, but I felt like I'd been kicked squarely in the balls, totally sickened and more or less told him to get out of the yard. I phoned the ICC offices later that day and asked to be put through to Jerry Desmond who was the Chairman at the time. I didn't get through and was asked what it was about. I told her that if there was ever a reoccurrence of what happened that day I'd drop all the dogs off at their offices and they could rear them.

I had a phone call from the rearer in Waterford asking if the pups were coming to him as if he didn't know there was any problem. Maybe he didn't, I can't say for certain, but I wasn't long about putting him straight on exactly why they weren't going, along with a warning that probably went unheeded.

Another couple of weeks passed without hearing from anyone. I believed that he'd no intention of paying me anything and that contacting the ICC was intended to frighten me into giving them to him. I did get a Solicitor's letter shortly after this, which again was intended to intimidate. I answered this with a letter request for the thirty-four hundred euro his client owed me and told him that his dogs were going to be rehomed if the bill wasn't paid within ten days. His Solicitor phoned me within the ten days asking what amount I'd be prepared to accept. I told him the only amount was the full amount. He kept trying at this until I stopped him. I asked him: "Is this coming from your client or you?" He told me it was his own doing and if he could get a settlement figure from me he'd go back to his client. "I know your client better than you and he's no intention of paying me or probably you either. You're in Dublin, he's in England. I doubt you'll get paid either". That was that.

A short time later I had the dogs adopted through registered greyhound adoption centres and got supporting paperwork from them. I know he got some of the pups back, through badgering the adoption centres and probably threatening them too, but I half-expected that. I was on a hiding to nothing, feeding them every week. The only consolation I could take was that none of the litter turned out to be any good despite their excellent breeding, rearing and good looks. I had whelped down and reared two litters practically for nothing. What's worse, is that space could have been used for others that I would have got paid for.

A lot of rearers in Ireland will take half of a litter as payment for rearing the other half for the breeder. It's an arrangement that suits both parties as there's no cash sum to be handed out in one go. This arrangement never interested me as I was breeding my own litters. Any dogs I took in for rearing was on a payment basis only and I never had any problems with anyone else not paying me. There will always be some who are a bit slow with it, but that's human nature. I know that the other rearer in Waterford had agreed to school all the pups for a half share in them and anything they might be worth.

Thoughts and opinions

The following is a mix mash of my thoughts and opinions regarding greyhounds. Following this is Appendix A which is an eBook that I wrote in 2005, titled "The Cost-Effective Way Of Breeding Greyhounds". You'll see that although written in 2005, the costs of many things listed in it are still very similar today. Pup prices for breeders are no better, yet stud fees and food costs have increased. Breeders now (2020) are worse off than ever before, yet trainers are enjoying more and more syndicates coming into the sport.

Luck

Some people will tell you that you make your own luck and that greyhounds make their own luck. I don't subscribe to this. As long as a dog is genuine, he needs a certain amount of luck to win the final of a big race. How many times do we see hot favourites beaten in finals because they miss the break or get bumped at the bend? If winning races wasn't so unpredictable, there wouldn't be any bookmakers willing to lay a bet. The biggest commodity in greyhounds is luck. When you breed, you don't know how the pups are going to turn out and you need luck in rearing them, and with injuries, and everything else. Luck seems to follow some and desert others. There're so many variables in greyhound racing and breeding, luck will always play a huge part.

The only brood bitch I paid a lot of money for was one named Tyone Sharon (Arrigle Buddy x Live Commentary), Live Commentary (Live Contender x Minnies Nikita). As you probably know, the Minnies line was prolific for producing champion greyhounds and Live Commentary was one of her best daughters on track and in the breeding paddocks. Tyone Sharon won the Consolation Final of the Irish St. Leger at Limerick and also won in 28.60 there when the track ran a lot slower than it does today. A litter brother, Killinan Buddy broke the TR for the sprint at Thurles and I reckoned this bitch was a certainty to produce good hounds. I paid two grand for her, in preference to a leasing deal for a dog and bitch from every litter. In hindsight, I should have taken the deal. The best dog she had was one I trained and had a half share in, named Mollys Champ (by Droopys Kewell). He only had a handful of races before serious injury, but he had impressive early pace and got injured in the final of an A3 stake at Longford when in front coming off the last bend, he had his heels clipped by the dog in second. It was all he could do, stop himself from falling and in the effort, he sustained a muscle injury that he never came back from. He had been improving in every run and had started to trap in his last two races. He was beaten a length and a short head in this final and was so unlucky. He was shaping up very nicely to make a really decent dog. He was extremely genuine and gutsy. She had other dogs that made minor open class to Toll Security and Elles Dominator too, but she was a disappointing brood overall.

Another disappointing brood I owned was Killavarrig Ruby that I got relatively cheaply. She was by Droopys Kewell x Rising Singer and a sister to the flying Goblet Of Fire and the whole litter were very good. Ruby herself broke the TR at Hull for 270M. Her litter sister Rising Angel produced Taylors Sky winner of the 2011 English Derby. Ruby's pups were disappointing to all the stud dogs she went to. Don't talk to me about luck!

Elles Dominator mated a bitch named Inky Black (Staplers Joe x Annies Bullet) who was fast and beautifully bred. The litter of five were okay and one of them was open class. Her previous litter to Sonic Flight were of similar ability. But, her third and last litter produced the 2006 Irish Derby winner Razldazl Billy (by Brett Lee).

In 2004, I was asked by an English owner to school a pup for him that he owned. The pup was bred and reared at Shelbourne stud and he was a big rangy, very impressive looking black pup. It soon became obvious when galloping him that he could run and seemed to have buckets of stamina with it. His first hand-slip couldn't have been more than two hundred yards and he smashed his hock. I'll never forget it as long as I live. The dog just came to a stop and sat down on the track, no crying or yelping or any sound. It was a horrible break with the bone sticking out all over the place and his owner decided the kindest thing was to put the dog to sleep. The rest of the litter were mostly top-class and his brother Trey United (Kiowa Sweet Trey x Lemon United) was a finalist in the Irish Derby and later stood at stud in America.

I had another bitch too, I got as a free brood that held a TR in England that wasn't in the place a day when she broke a back leg in the paddock. I was owed a pup from a leasing deal at twelve months and picked out this lovely looking brindled son of Toll Security, having travelled to Galway and back to get him and he managed to break a leg also within a couple of days of arriving.

Anyone who has handled a large kennel of greyhounds will be able to relate with similar tales. It's part and parcel of the game and dogs will always get hurt and accidents will happen no matter how careful you are, but anyone that says luck has nothing to do with it hasn't a clue what they're talking about. It's such a fickle game, that chance will always play a huge part in every aspect of it. Otherwise, bookmakers would never make any money.

Stud keepers

I'd like to see all stud-keepers implement a full refund policy when there are no pups resulting from a mating, or better still, a policy of pay-when-you-pup. I don't think it's as bad today as it was twenty years ago, but many breeders are told a mating took place when it didn't and charged accordingly. I sent a bitch down to Tucks Mein one time and I was told that the bitch would only stand for one mating (rather than the two I wanted) and I thought I was being misled when I asked questions about it. The bitch missed and I never got to use the so-called 'free service' that I was entitled to. The 'free service' system should be abolished forever and a 100% refund should be implemented for missing bitches across the full spectrum of stud-keepers with no exceptions for natural matings and the use of AI. I also think in the case of frozen implants that there needs to be a better system too than the breeder only receiving a free straw in the event of a missing bitch.

Transparency within the powers that be

There needs to be greater transparency in the dealings of the IGB and the ICC. Control stewards are not supposed to own greyhounds themselves for obvious implications and reasons, yet every one of them I've known have owned dogs and some were openly acting as agents, buying and selling dogs, whilst carrying out their official duties. The people being appointed important positions within both of these organisations often leave a lot to be desired and often are selected due to having friends in the right places, rather than being the best candidates for the job. No son or daughter of a professional trainer should be given positions as racing managers or control stewards, as has happened. I'd like to see all brood bitches being registered and blood tested the same as the stud dogs are, as I believe a large percentage of the studbook is probably wrong.

Small greyhounds

This is a problem that often stays under the radar within the greyhound industry. Many greys are born that end up simply too small to become racers. A few years ago, I wanted a small greyhound bitch to breed to a champion Whippet for a litter of Grews (Greyhound x Whippet) for straight-line lurcher racing. These are very useful dogs especially in racing categories that are chosen by height. I put an ad up on Greyhound-data and was amazed at the number of replies I got offering me diminutive bitches, all for free. Some of them were extremely well-bred from top stud dogs and brood bitches, but all failed to make the grade due to being too small. They were all from forty to forty-seven pounds if I remember rightly and I got about thirty replies. If one advert yielded such a response at any one time, I think it's fair to say that the same advert at any time would yield a similar response. I bred a small line of greyhounds myself through Racefield Kate (Game Ball x Raymonds Pride), but they were all fifty pounds plus in weight (with one exception) and more importantly their size didn't stop them from winning. Sometimes small pups result from breeding small bitches, but more often it's the cross that sometimes suffers this size impediment and the resultant mix of bloodlines. Thirty years ago, you heard of dogs being small due to bad rearing and feeding, but regardless of whether this was true, I don't believe it happens today.

Greyhounds as pets/adoption

Greyhounds can make great pets as well as race dogs. This was hammered home to me when I visited Finland in 2006. The dogs there share the family home and go racing and trialling the same as any other racing greyhound. Most too, when they finish racing are kept on as pets for the end of their days. I think it's fair to say that in Ireland, no racing greys are kept in the home, nor double as pets and companions and most people keeping greyhounds here would think that the dogs wouldn't adapt to a household existence and would literally wreck the house. There is some truth to this as pups reared in a paddock all of their lives become institutionalised to a degree and many couldn't adapt to this. In Finland, most greyhounds are bought at twelve weeks, so the transition is a much smoother and easier one and they learn house-training the same as any other breed. Living in the home makes them much cleaner than the average paddock reared pup as you can imagine, without the muck and wet conditions that are part and parcel of puppy rearing in paddocks and so-called full freedom rearing in Ireland. Dogs are very adaptable animals and greyhounds are no exception to this. Living in the home limits the numbers that can be kept to one or two dogs, but I wouldn't have believed how they thrived in a home environment if I hadn't seen it, and I saw it in many homes there. The extra attention they got from living predominantly as pets enabled them to bond with their owners as would most other breeds and appeared to have no detrimental effects when taken racing. To see them curled up in front of the fire after racing in the living-room, said it all.

Everyone now, I think, accepts that there are some great adoption agencies for retired greyhounds and these dogs get to live out their days as a pet by an owner that genuinely cares for them. It also shows that even after a conventional rearing and racing life over three or four years, they can still adapt to life in a pet home. Not all adoption agencies though are equal. There's very little legislation in Ireland involved in setting up a charity and they only have to donate 20% of profits to a charitable cause, so this is open to rampant misinterpretation in charities as a whole, not only animal ones. Unfortunately, some greyhound adoption centres are running for-profit and are run as money-making businesses under the guise of a charity. I dropped off a couple of dogs one time at one of these places and took the dogs home again as the place was filthy and very badly run. There cannot be enough genuine adoption centres that only have the dog's welfare in pole position.

Practically no-one buys greyhound pups as pets. A lucky few will become pets after an injury as a pup, but generally speaking, this happens very rarely. Breed books and dog psychologists rate the intelligence of greyhounds as amongst the lowest of all breeds, but this is unfair as well as untrue. The typical rearing of a greyhound does little, I feel, to promote learning and intelligence within a pup, compared to a pet breed that's living with a family from eight weeks of age. The commonly believed sagacity of lurchers in contrast to greyhounds is a fallacy in most cases, and in my opinion, the only difference in potential intelligence is in the rearing. Lurchers typically live more of a pet existence and spend much more time with their owners than greyhounds. It's accepted by animal psychologists that the crucial learning phase for any dog is between four and sixteen weeks of age. Any dog that doesn't have adequate human handling and attention (during this period) suffers in his social and emotional development. Don't get me wrong, anyone rearing large numbers of greyhounds can only do it as they've always done by catering for large numbers as best they can and this way will prepare them for racing life and possibly a lucrative one. What I'm saying is that I believe this type of rearing does little for the individual intelligence of any dog and I believe that the greyhound is a very intelligent breed, given the chance to become so. You only have to look at the track-craft that some dogs have to see this, despite their rearing and relatively little human attention. The greyhound thrives on human company and attention.

The greyhound has as much to offer as a pet and companion as any other breed. The greatest danger is their propensity to chase or kill small game or anything they see as small game, such as small dogs and cats. They can be trained though not to do this or at least trained to differentiate. They can be obedience trained too, but again this is often more difficult than with other more accepted pet breeds. Again, I think rearing plays a part in this. If kept as pets from an early age, their aptitude for training and learning would be greatly magnified and increased. Any dog, particularly from the hound family needs careful recall training as the hunting instinct can be very strong.

I know if I had set up my kennels to breed Yorkshire Terriers, Westies, and Cavalier King Charles spaniels instead of Greyhounds, it would have been a lot easier and a lot more lucrative. They also would have eaten a lot less! When you can buy a well-bred greyhound for half the price of some of the above-mentioned breeds, there's something drastically wrong with the greyhound industry. The saddest thing is that it's been this way for many years and seems unlikely to change for the better.

Chasing/Non-chasing

I believe that as much as 20% of greyhounds bred do not chase properly and it's a huge problem for breeders as the dogs are worthless when this is realised.

People

Most people you meet in most walks of life are genuine for the most part, but there are always exceptions and some people's expectations are unreasonable.

I remember a local guy called Joe Price made contact with me after following my postings on the internet. Although he was local, I didn't know him prior to this. Initially, he asked me what dog meal I was using and bought some from me. After this, he started to call into the kennels every now and then just to chat. He was a bookmaker at Mullingar track and he'd just set up a kennel facility on his own property for his youngest daughter to have a go at training greyhounds. He seemed to like the way I ran my kennel.

One day he asked me if I had anything unraced that had potential. I told him I had a pup that I liked the look of, but he'd only had a hand-slip and it was too soon to know much more about him. He asked to see the dog who was a son of Toll Security x Moyar Mist (this bitch I bought from England when finished racing as she was a daughter Westmead Gigi and grand-daughter of Westmead Chick). He asked me if I thought he would be good and how much I wanted for him. I said I fancied him, but it was early days and I wanted 1250 for him as he was. He wanted to see the dog running, so I agreed to slip him behind another pup at Mullingar that I knew he'd pick up easily enough so he could see the dog going past another dog cleanly. As I said, this was only the dog's second hand-slip. The pup impressed him and he bought him. A few months later, however, he rang me and expressed disappointment that the pup hadn't turned out as good as he had hoped. I said: "Well, that's greyhound racing," and asked him if the pup had turned out better than he'd hoped, would he be phoning me? The dog was genuine and won a couple of races, but was only average. I knew he was looking for some sort of compensation without asking for it outright, but I felt justified in offering nothing as I felt the pup hadn't been overpriced. I heard little from him afterwards, clearly, he wasn't happy.

Another local guy mated a bitch to Toll Security but she suddenly died in the kennel about two weeks before she was to have her pups. He rang me, a farmer named Danny, and he was nearly in tears over the loss of the bitch and the litter. It just so happened, I had a bitch in the kennel also due to whelp in the near future and I offered her to him in return for two pups from the litter at 12 weeks and the bitch back at the same time. He accepted this (Funtime Fliss was the name of the bitch) and was clearly delighted with this arrangement. The bitch had a decent sized litter and they turned out pretty decent too. I had plenty of pups at the time and although not under any obligation, I felt this was the right thing to do in the circumstances.

One of my owners, Kieran Boles, bought two pups by Token Prince out of a decent Irish bred bitch and they came to me when ready for schooling. A dog and a bitch, the dog had pace but I quickly saw he wasn't genuine. Kieran was very pragmatic and didn't want to be paying for a dog that couldn't potentially pay his way. I happened to mention to a guy that bought pups from me that the dog was available for free and he jumped at the chance to take him and he put him with an owner of a small private track to try and get him chasing properly. A few months later, the dog won a puppy race in Dundalk in 29.20 and was sold for a decent sum. He was also handled by a professional trainer and a large gamble was enjoyed on the night by connections afterwards. Kieran was annoyed that the guy that took the dog for free didn't tell him or me that the dog was worth backing. The dog didn't win another race afterwards and I believe went back to his erratic chasing habits.

Another time, I took a dog to train from an English couple living near Tralee in Kerry. The dog only stayed 500 yards max and they were having difficulty at their local track getting races for him either over 500 or the sprint distance. They believed he was top class over any two bend distance and was a contender for any open sprint race. They were wrong. He was a decent A1/S1 dog, but in my opinion, was a couple of lengths off being open class. He ran in a very hot open sprint at Dundalk but failed to show. He also ran in an open race at Longford and didn't show there either. I did manage a win in his third race over 400 at Mullingar in 21.70 which was a good, if not great, time. This was a top-grade race and I believe this was the dog's limit. The owners disagreed and ended up taking him back as I didn't want to be taking the dog around the country to races that I felt he wasn't good enough to win.

Postscript

Today, I have much involvement with dogs of various breeds, but very little involvement with greyhounds. I grew extremely disillusioned after the issue with the large kennel bill I was stuck with as I've described in the last chapter and I developed a back problem that eventually curtailed what I could physically do. The writing was on the wall as I too had lost much of my enthusiasm due to the heavy workload and never-ending cycle of what a large kennel entails. After a break from greyhounds, I studied to become a dog behaviourist and obedience trainer. This, in turn, led me to take on dogs with behavioural problems and rehabilitating them in a short time period. My natural confidence in handling dogs undoubtedly comes from, at least in part, handling hundreds of greyhounds of all ages, sizes and temperaments. I also became interested in tracking training with dogs and have two excellent people-tracking dogs here that I've trained myself.

The one thing that has always been a constant in my life has been my love of working with and spending time with dogs. This will never change as long as I live and applies to all dogs, all breeds and all shapes and sizes.

I hope you've enjoyed this read of my experiences and if you fancy giving greyhounds a go fulltime, I hope it will make you think of the pitfalls and challenges that will lie ahead, should you pursue this endeavour. I don't consider myself any more of an expert than anyone else and I wrote this account as I realised that I was beginning to forget many things from the past and I wanted to get the memories down on paper to preserve them for my kids. When I let some friends read it, they encouraged me to print it and make it available for the general public. I've many more stories that either I can't remember sufficiently or I've made many mistakes during my time in greyhounds, but I did the best I could and have only a few regrets. For the most part, I loved it.

The following is an Ebook I wrote in 2005 and it's been a free download on greyhound-data since then. Some of it is still as relevant today as when it was written, some of it fifteen years later is dated. You can make your own mind up. It does cover some of the brood bitches I got for little or nothing and goes some way to explaining how I built up a breeding kennel as quickly and as cost-effectively as I did.

Best Regards,

Mark Telford

Appendix A

FOREWORD

by Mark Telford (copyright Mark Telford) 2005

THIS EBOOK CAME ABOUT DUE TO TWO DIFFERENT EVENTS, BOTH OF WHICH MADE ME THINK. THE FIRST EVENT CAME ABOUT WHEN A MAN OF ABOUT SEVENTY CAME AND BOUGHT 4 PUPS FROM ME RECENTLY. HE BOUGHT TWO PUPS OVER THE PHONE AND ASKED ME TO PICK THEM OUT FOR HIM; THEY WERE DELIVERED TO HIM VIA GREYHOUND TRANSPORT TO LIFFORD TRACK. HE WAS SO DELIGHTED WITH THE PUPS HE CAME BACK IN PERSON A FEW DAYS LATER AND BOUGHT TWO MORE AND WE CHATTED ABOUT THIS AND THAT, ALL TO DO WITH DOGS.

HE TOLD ME HE'D BEEN VERY IMPRESSED HOW WELL THE PUPS LOOKED, IN PARTICULAR THEIR SHINY COATS AND THE 'GREAT BACKS' ON THEM. HE ASKED ME

WHAT BRAND OF DOG MEAL OR NUTS I USED AND COULDN'T BELIEVE THE LOW PRICE IT CAN BE BOUGHT AT, GIVEN ITS OBVIOUS QUALITY (MORE ABOUT THIS LATER). HE ASKED ME WHAT I USED ON MY DOGS TO ELIMINATE FLEAS AS HE HAD PREVIOUSLY USED THE VERY EXPENSIVE AND INEFFECTIVE 'FRONTLINE' PRODUCT SOLD BY VETS, WHICH SELLS FOR APPROX 24 EUROS (£16)AND ONLY EFFECTIVELY WASHES ABOUT 3 DOGS (FAR TOO EXPENSIVE TO USE IF YOU WANT TO WASH MAYBE 25 OR 30), AND HE'D ALSO USED THE 'SPOT ON' VIALS WHICH WORK OUT ABOUT 10 EUROS(£7) PER DOG; TOO EXPENSIVE FOR A KENNEL FULL OF DOGS.

I SHOWED HIM A BOTTLE OF CLEAR LIQUID THAT WHEN MIXED WITH WATER I GUARANTEED HIM WOULD BE SUFFICIENT TO WASH AND RID MAYBE 90 DOGS OF FLEAS. THE COST? A MERE 8.50 EURO (UNDER £6). (MORE ABOUT THIS LATER). HE WENT AWAY AND BOUGHT A LARGER BOTTLE AND SENT ME DOWN HALF OF IT COS HE RECKONED HE HAD SO MUCH OF IT, HE WOULDN'T LIVE LONG ENOUGH TO USE IT ALL. (I KID YOU NOT!) COST £14(21 EUROS).

THE SECOND EVENT WAS A DISCUSSION ON GLOBAL GREYHOUNDS (GG) UNDER THE HEADING "COSTS OF BREEDING" WHICH WAS A VERY INTERESTING TOPIC WITH MANY WORTHY CONTRIBUTORS. THE TOPIC WAS INITIATED BY PUP72, WHO AMONGST OTHER THINGS MENTIONED THAT I HAD TOLD HIM SEVERAL MONTHS PREVIOUSLY THAT HE WOULD HAVE TO SELL 5 PUPS OF HIS RECENT LITTER BY DROOPYS KEWELL JUST TO COVER HIS BASIC BREEDING COSTS (NOT LEAST THE 1000 EURO STUD FEE, THE SAME DOG IS NOW 1200), TO BREAK EVEN. AT THE TIME HE RECKONED THIS COULD BE ACCOMPLISHED BY SELLING JUST 2 PUPS. HE SAYS IN THE TOPIC THAT I WAS 'ACTUALLY RIGHT' IN MY PREDICTION OF 5.

OTHER THINGS COVERED IN THE THREADS WERE HOW DIFFICULT IT HAS BECOME TO SELL PUPS, OR RATHER TO GET 'DECENT' PRICES FOR PUPS AS THERE ARE SO MANY FOR SALE RIGHT NOW AT VERY REASONABLE PRICES. VERY FEW PEOPLE TRY TO EARN A LIVING FROM BREEDING GREYHOUNDS, FOR MOST IT'S A HOBBY FUNDED BY MORE REGULAR EMPLOYMENT. MOST PEOPLE HOPE TO SELL OFF MOST OF

THE LITTER, TO COVER THEIR COSTS AND KEEP 1 OR 2 FOR THEMSELVES. FACT IS, AT THIS PARTICULAR MOMENT IN TIME AND THE CURRENT STATE OF THE DOGGY GAME, IT HAS BECOME INCREASINGLY HARDER TO DO THIS. PUPS CAN'T BE SOLD AT 'RESPECTABLE PRICES' ANY MORE, THEY WON'T SELL NOWADAYS

IRRESPECTIVE OF HOW WELL BRED THEY ARE UNLESS THEY'RE REASONABLY PRICED.

MAIN REASONS FOR THIS ARE, AS I SEE IT, THE LACK OF INTEREST AND SUBSEQUENT DROP IN VALUE OF THE AVERAGE GRADER, AND THERE ARE JUST TOO MANY PUPS FOR SALE, MORE THAN THE DEMAND REQUESTS IN THE CURRENT MARKETPLACE.

I'VE BEEN INVOLVED IN GREYHOUNDS ALL MY LIFE, SINCE A YOUNG LAD, BUT IT'S ONLY IN THE LAST TWO YEARS THAT I PLUCKED UP THE COURAGE TO PACK IN MY DECENT PAYING SALES JOB, AND MAKE A LIVING FULLTIME BREEDING AND REARING GREYHOUNDS. I AM 34 NOW. DURING THIS TIME, I HAVE BRED NUMEROUS LITTERS, WHICH I HAVE SOLD VERY WELL AT REASONABLE PRICES (SOME PEOPLE SAY 'CRAZY PRICES') AND MOST IMPORTANTLY,

I'VE MADE A LIVING FOR MY FAMILY AND I DOING SO.

THE PURPOSE OF THIS EBOOK IS TO SHOW PEOPLE HOW I DO IT, AND BY DOING THE SAME ITS POSSIBLE FOR ANYONE TO CUT THEIR COSTS OF BREEDING A LITTER, WHICH ENABLES THEM TO ACCEPT A LOWER ASKING PRICE FOR THEIR PUPS AT SALE TIME AND STILL AT LEAST COVER THEIR COSTS IF NOT MAKE A LITTLE MONEY.

I JUST WANT TO SAY A WORD OR TWO BEFORE I START INTO THE CONTENT PROPER. BY WRITING THIS I AM NOT PUTTING MYSELF FORWARD AS AN EXPERT OR AN AUTHORITY ON ANY ASPECT OF GREYHOUNDS. THIS EBOOK CONSISTS OF MY THEORIES AND OPINIONS BASED ON MY EXPERIENCES AND LEARNINGS FROM WORKING WITH AND BREEDING THESE WONDERFUL ANIMALS.

I DO NOT HAVE ANY VETERINARY TRAINING (I HAVE OFTEN WONDERED THE SAME ABOUT NUMEROUS VETS!!!) AND ANYTHING I HAVE ADMINISTERED AS STATED IN THIS WRITING IS EXACTLY AS I SAY. I AM NOT QUALIFIED TO GIVE VETERINARY ADVICE

AND AM NOT DOING SO. NOR DO I ACCEPT ANY RESPONSIBILITY OR BLAME IF ANYONE USES THE INFORMATION I GIVE, WITH UNSATISFACTORY RESULTS. WHAT I DO AND STATE HAS WORKED FOR ME, WHICH IS THE REASON I DO IT. I DO NOT SEEK TO INFLUENCE ANYONE ELSES ACTIONS.

PEOPLE ARE QUITTING THE BREEDING GAME BY THE DOZEN BECAUSE THEY THINK IT'S JUST NOT PAYING. I TEND TO THINK IT STILL PAYS BUT YOU NEED TO PLAY BY DIFFERENT RULES MAYBE THAN IN THE PAST. I WILL INEVITABLY IMPART SOME OF MY IDEAS REGARDING BREEDING AS I EXPLAIN MY REASONING FOR SOME OF MY THINKING THROUGHOUT THIS TEXT, AGAIN I'M NOT PUTTING MYSELF FORWARD AS AN EXPERT.

I HAVEN'T BRED ENOUGH LITTERS OR ENOUGH CLASS PERFORMERS, IN MY OPINION, TO QUALIFY AS THAT. I HAVE CONFIDENCE IN MY JUDGEMENT AND MY ABILITY IN THE WORK THAT I DO WITH MY GREYHOUNDS. LIKE MOST BREEDERS I HAVE BRED GOOD AND BAD DOGS AND MORE BAD THAN GOOD. I'M LESS THAN 2 YEARS INTO A CURRENT 10 YEAR BREEDING

PLAN THAT I MAPPED OUT SOME TIME AGO, WE'LL SEE HOW THAT GOES IN TIME. WHAT THIS BOOK IS ABOUT IS BREEDING PUPS AS WELL AS POSSIBLE BY CUTTING COSTS, YET NOT CUTTING QUALITY IN ANYTHING, BE IT FOOD, BLOODLINES, OR

GENERAL DAY-TO-DAY CARE.

WHY BREED?

I BREED BECAUSE I WANT TO ESTABLISH LINES THAT WILL BE IDENTIFIED AS MINE. I'D RATHER BE KNOWN AS THE BREEDER OF A DERBY WINNER THAN THE TRAINER (IF NOT BOTH!!). IN THE PAST FEW MONTHS I HAVE SOLD PUPS ALL OVER IRELAND AND WILL LOOK FORWARD TO HOPEFULLY READING ABOUT THEIR WINS TO COME AT MANY TRACKS. IN MOST CASES I WILL STILL HAVE THE DAM IN THE KENNEL AND MAYBE ANOTHER LITTER FROM HER FOLLOWING ON, SO I AWAIT WITH GREAT HOPE AND INTEREST. WITH PUPS THERE IS SO MUCH HOPE AND POTENTIAL, TWO PUPS SIDE BY SIDE AT 12

WEEKS, ONE COULD BE A STAR AND THE OTHER A BOTTOM GRADER. NOBODY

KNOWS AND NOBODY CAN TELL WITH ANY DEGREE OF RELIABILITY WHO WILL BE THE BETTER. THEY CAN BE A DELIGHT OR ONE HELL OF A DISAPPOINTMENT AND A LOT OF GREY IN

BETWEEN, BUT FOR ME, ALL BREEDERS ARE DREAMERS TO A CERTAIN EXTENT (UNLESS THEY'RE IN IT SOLELY TO MAKE MONEY, AND 99.9% OF THESE TYPES WON'T), AND PUPS KEEP YOU DREAMING!

BROODBITCHES

I THINK THE BROOD IS MUCH MORE IMPORTANT THAN THE SIRE, IF SHE HASN'T GOT THE GENETIC EQUIPMENT TO PASS ON, NO SIRE WILL MAKE A DIFFERENCE. EVERYBODY WANTS TO HAVE A TOP BROODBITCH BUT THEY'RE HARD TO FIND AND IT TAKES HER TO HAVE 2-3 LITTERS REALISTICALLY BEFORE YOU KNOW HOW GOOD SHE IS, IF ANY GOOD AT ALL.

I LIKE TO TAKE A CHANCE ON A YOUNG MAIDEN BITCH, FROM TOP

BLOODLINES, PREFERABLY FROM A GOOD LITTER AND SOME WINNING FORM FOR HER. IF SHE'S OPEN CLASS HERSELF THAT'S

A BONUS BUT NOT CRUCIAL TO ME IF WELL ENOUGH BRED AS I BELIEVE THAT GREYHOUNDS SOMETIMES SKIP A GENERATION GENETICALLY WHEN IT COMES TO REPRODUCING FAST DOGS. THAT'S WHY MANY BROODS WHO WERE UNRACED OR POOR RACERS THEMSELVES, BUT FROM GREAT DAMS OFTEN PRODUCE THE GOODS. IN SHORT, I FAVOUR BREEDING AS IMPORTANT AS RACING ABILITY WHEN SELECTING

A POTENTIAL BROOD. IF YOU CAN GET A BITCH WITH BOTH ABILITY AND BREEDING, YOU HAVE A VERY GOOD BET INDEED, AS LONG AS SHE HASN'T BEEN OVERRACED AS I BELIEVE THIS TO BE A DETRIMENT TO HER POTENTIAL. OBVIOUSLY, IF SHE WAS FAST HERSELF IT IMPROVES YOUR CHANCES OF BREEDING FAST PUPS.

IF SHE COULD RUN A BIT, I WOULDN'T WORRY TOO MUCH WHAT HER DISTANCE PREFERENCES WERE, WHETHER A SPRINTER, MIDDLE DISTANCE, OR A STAYING BITCH. ANOTHER GOOD BET IS A BITCH THAT IS A LITTER SISTER TO A TOP CLASS DOG OR MEMBER OF A REALLY GOOD LITTER, EVEN IF THE BITCH HERSELF WASN'T ALL THAT

FAST(AS LONG AS SHE WAS GENUINE). IF YOU KEEP MATING TOP CLASS BLOODLINES TOGETHER, SOONER OR LATER YOU

WILL HIT THE JACKPOT AND PRODUCE CLASS. I FIRMLY BELIEVE THAT AND IT'S POSSIBLE TO DO THAT WITHOUT SPENDING A FORTUNE AS I WILL SHOW YOU.

WHAT ABOUT JUST BUYING A PROVEN BROOD?

WELL, YOU COULD IF YOU CAN FIND ONE FOR SALE AND YOU HAD A LARGE WAD OF CASH TO PART WITH, AND AS THIS EBOOK IS ABOUT CUTTING COSTS I DON'T RECOMMEND IT.

FURTHERMORE, A PROVEN BROOD OFFERED FOR SALE WILL LIKELY BE QUITE OLD AND HER FERTILITY MAY HAVE DECLINED (WHICH MIGHT BE THE REASON SHES FOR SALE). SHE MIGHT HAVE MISSED ON HER LAST MATING OR TWO, OR PRODUCED VERY FEW PUPS OF LATE.

I'D BE VERY CAREFUL ABOUT BUYING AN AGING BROOD WITHOUT LOOKING INTO THESE FACTORS.

IF YOU HAD A BROOD THAT YOU'D BRED A FEW TIMES WITH GREAT SUCCESS, WHY WOULD YOU SELL HER? UNLESS SOMEONE HAS A GENUINE REASON, AND SOMETIMES THEY DO EXIST, (NEEDING MONEY, MOVING HOUSE, FAILING HEALTH, OWNER AGING HIMSELF, ETC) I'D BE RELUCTANT TO PURCHASE SUCH A BITCH. YOU COULD OFFER TO LEASE SUCH A BITCH FOR SALE, WITH A GUARANTEE THAT

YOU'D AUTOMATICALLY BUY HER ONCE SHE PRODUCED A HEALTHY LITTER FOR YOU AT FIRST TIME OF TRYING. THAT MIGHT GIVE YOU SOME OF THE ANSWERS TO MY CONCERNS ABOVE AND TELL

YOU SOMETHING ABOUT THE INTEGRITY OF THE OWNER AS WELL.

WHY CHOOSE A MAIDEN BITCH?

FOR MANY REASONS, MOSTLY POSITIVE ONES.

SHES YOUNG FOR ONE THING(IF SHES NOT I WOULDN'T TAKE HER OVER AGE 5, SHE MAY HAVE BEEN TRIED BEFORE AND HAVE PROBLEMS CONCEIVING). SHE'S LIKELY TO BE MORE FERTILE THAN AN OLDER BITCH. A

BITCH BETWEEN 2 AND 3 YEARS OF AGE THAT COMES IN SEASON EVERY 6 MTHS IS PERFECT TO TAKE A CHANCE WITH. YOU CAN BREED HER FOR 2-3 LITTERS AND SHES STILL RELATIVELY YOUNG. THEN YOU CAN WAIT IF NEED BE TO SEE WHAT HER PROGENY ARE LIKE BEFORE COMMITTING YOURSELF TO BREEDING HER AGAIN.

I ALSO THINK THAT IF A BITCH HAS ABILITY AS A BROOD, THEY'RE BETTER THE YOUNGER THEY ARE. I THINK LITTER QUALITY POSSIBLY DECLINES AS THE BITCH ADVANCES IN YEARS (ALONG WITH LITTER SIZE). MANY BREEDERS THINK THE FIRST 3 LITTERS A BITCH HAS ARE HER BEST.

MOST IMPORTANT REASON FOR USING A MAIDEN BITCH?

THEY CAN BE GOT FOR VERY LITTLE AND MORE OFTEN FOR

NOTHING... YES, THAT'S A FACT! ANYTHING I TELL YOU IN THIS EBOOK IS BACKED UP BY MY EXPERIENCE. MANY, MANY NGRC BITCHES IN PARTICULAR, BUT ALSO IRISH RACERS TOO WHEN THEY

FINISH RACING ARE GIVEN AWAY BECAUSE THE OWNERS DON'T WANT TO BREED, OR NEVER HAVE BRED A LITTER IN THEIR LIVES.

MOST RACERS WHEN THEIR CAREER IS OVER AREN'T WANTED AND ARE REHOMED OR WHATEVER.

ONLY TOP CLASS, GROUP WINNING OR CONTENDING BITCHES ARE SOUGHT AFTER AND WILL EXCHANGE HANDS FOR DECENT MONEY.

THE REST ARE GIVEN AWAY TO GOOD HOMES. (IF NOT RACING, THEIR KENNEL BILLS STILL HAVE TO BE PAID, SO THEY'RE GLADLY GIVEN AWAY TO A GOOD HOME) THIS IS ONE INSTANCE WHERE THE CURRENTLY POOR MARKET FOR SELLING GREYHOUND PUPS WORKS TO YOUR ADVANTAGE. YOU CAN GET WELL-BRED BITCHES, SOMETIMES OPEN CLASS INTO THE BARGAIN FOR NOTHING, OR SOMETIMES IN EXCHANGE FOR 1 PUP FROM HER FIRST LITTER.

IF THERE WERE MORE PEOPLE BREEDING THERE WOULD BE MORE DEMAND FOR THESE BITCHES AND FEWER AVAILABLE. ONE THING GOING IN YOUR FAVOUR

REGARDING THESE BITCHES AND THE REASON THEY'RE SO EASILY OBTAINED IS THAT MANY PEOPLE WHO SEE' SOMETHING IS FREE' HAVE A SUBCONSCIOUS BELIEF THAT 'IF IT'S FREE, IT COULDN'T BE ANY GOOD' AND AS A RESULT IGNORE SUCH ADVERTS. THIS IS TRUE, PARTICULARLY IN IRELAND, BUT IT

APPLIES EVERYWHERE AND PART OF A GENERAL MENTALITY THAT PREDOMINATES IN GREYHOUND CIRCLES.

IT IS VERY EASY TO SLIP INTO THIS WAY OF THINKING, BUT THOSE WHO FOLLOW THEIR OWN MIND AND GUT INSTINCT WILL SUCCEED WHERE OTHERS FAIL.

EXAMPLES

THE FOLLOWING BITCHES I OBTAINED FOR NOTHING IN MOST CASES.

1 OF THEM I PAID £500 FOR(THE MOST I'VE EVER PAID), 2 OF THEM WAS IN EXCHANGE FOR A PUP AT 12WEEKS, AND ONE WAS OBTAINED FOR A STRAIGHT SWAP FOR A 12-MONTH-OLD SAPLING. THE REST WERE COMPLETELY FREE.

RACEFIELD SHELLY (http://www.greyhound-data.com/d?i=1075853) WON 4 FROM 7 FROM A6 TO NGRC OPEN CLASS, BROKE WRIST IN LAST RACE. MEMBER OF A VERY GOOD LITTER. DAM DAVITT FLASH WAS DERBY CLASS WINNER OF MANY OPENS(27.70 460M WIMBLEDON), AND SISTER TO REDWOOD SARA(WINNER 2 CLASSICS AND DAM OF RUMMY LAD). GRAND-DAM REDWOOD GIRL WON 2 CLASSICS AND DAM OF MANY MANY TOP PERFORMERS.

FUNTIME FLISS (http://www.greyhound-data.com/d?i=477196) WINNER OF 12 RACES, A2 CLASS 465M BELLEVUE. SUFFERED FROM CRAMPING. HER RECORD SHOWS SHE LED IN NEARLY ALL HER RACES AND HER 1ST SECTIONAL TIMES WERE ON PAR WITH THE LAST 3 TR FOR COURSE AND DISTANCE. SHE'S VERY SIMILARLY BRED TO DOUBLE DERBY WINNER 'REACTABOND REBEL' AND ALSO LAURELS WINNER AND STUD DOG 'EL PREMIER'.

HANNAHS RIBBON (http://www.greyhound-data.com/d?i=526664)

THIS BITCH WON 18 TOP GRADE FLAPPING RACES AND RECORDED 16.40,16.50 AT HINCKLEY FOR 300 WHICH ARE CRACKING TIMES. HER DAM HAS PRODUCED MANY SUB 29 SEC DOGS IN IRELAND. H/RIBBON'S BROTHER XAMAX RUGRAT WON MANY OPENS AND LED SONIC FLIGHT IN 2ND ROUND OF ENG DERBY.

HAZY TEX (http://www.greyhound-data.com/d?i=342002) WON 8 RACES, A2 GRADE SUNDERLAND 450M. SISTER TO PINEAPPLE EURO WINNER

GROUP 3 EVENT AT PBORO AND MANY, MANY OPEN RACES, ANOTHER BROTHER WAS PERRY BARR TRACK CHAMP AND CLOCKED 28.60,28.70. TEX'S DAM PINEAPPLE MANDY IS HOLDER OF THE TR AT TRALEE FOR 325 SINCE '99 AND DAM OF LANCE PINEAPPLE (MASTERS AND PBORO DERBY FINALIST) AND THROWS TOP CLASS IN EVERY LITTER. THIS DAMLINE HAS PRODUCED THE LIKES OF FLAGSTAR, PAGAN PINE AND

PINEAPPLE LEMON. SUPERB UNBROKEN DAMLINE CHAIN RIGHT BACK AT LEAST 6 GENERATIONS.

MOYAR MIST (http://www.greyhound-data.com/d?i=901626) WESTMEAD BREEDING, OUT OF DUAL OAKS FINALIST WESTMEAD GIGI.GRAND-

DAUGHTER OF WESTMEAD CHICK WHO IS A DAUGHTER OF WESTMEAD MOVE, GOING BACK THROUGH A LINE OF CHAMPION DAMS OF THE YEAR, WESTMEAD TANIA, WESTMEAD SATIN AND HACKSAW.

KILLAVARRIG RUBY (http://www.greyhound-data.com/d?i=886756) BROKE TR 270M AT HULL. WINNER OF MANY OPENS IN SCOTLAND ON FLAPS ALSO, PRACTICALLY UNBEATABLE UP TO 300 YARDS. MEMBER OF ALL OPEN CLASS LITTER INCLUDING THE FLYING 'GOBLET OF FIRE' LAURELS RUNNER-UP, LED TYRUR TED TO THIRD BEND. GOBLET OF FIRE CLOCKED 28.57 SHEL AND 28.30 CORK AMONGST MANY OTHER FINE WINS.

IM SURE YOU CAN SEE THE QUALITY OF THE ABOVE BREEDING THAT IS AVAILABLE FOR LITTLE OR NOTHING

I HAVE SINCE TURNED DOWN MANY OTHERS OF EQUAL/GREATER POTENTIAL, AND BREEDING DUE TO LACK OF SPACE.

WHERE TO FIND THESE MAIDEN BITCHES?

MANY ARE FOUND IN THE CLASSIFIEDS, MISCELLANEOUS SECTION ON GREYHOUND DATA WWW.GREYHOUND-DATA.COM.

OFTEN YOU WILL SEE THEM ADVERTISED IN THE SMALL ADS IN THE RACING POST, AND TO A LESSER EXTENT IN THE SPORTING PRESS, GREYHOUND WEEKLY, AND GREYHOUND STAR. OFTENTIMES THEY'RE PUT UP ON THE CLASSIFIEDS ON GLOBAL GREYHOUNDS, CHECK

PARTICULARLY THE UK SECTION. IF YOU KNOW ANY NGRC TRAINERS, ASK THEM TO KEEP YOU IN MIND FOR FUTURE DECENT BITCHES, WHEN THEY'VE FINISHED RACING AS MANY OWNERS WILL GLADLY

GIVE THEM TO YOU FREE OF CHARGE.

IMPORTANT POINT

MANY TIMES BITCHES WILL BE LISTED WITH JUST THEIR FIRST GENERATION PEDIGREE, SO ITS UP TO YOU TO DO YOUR HOMEWORK AND SPOT 'GOOD BREEDING' OR AT LEAST RESEARCH THE PEDIGREE ON

GREYHOUND-DATA IF YOU DON'T WANT TO MISS OUT. GREYHOUND-DATA IS A SUPER RESEARCH TOOL AND IS FREE OF

CHARGE, SO MAKE USE OF IT. MANY OWNER'S GIVING AWAY THESE BITCHES DON'T KNOW HOW WELL BRED THEY ARE, SO THE TIME YOU SPEND STUDYING AND RESEARCHING PEDIGREES COULDN'T BE

BETTER SPENT. HERE'S AN EXAMPLE OF EXACTLY WHAT I MEAN.

I BOUGHT A BITCH ONE TIME IN 1990, FIRST BROOD I EVER BOUGHT FROM AN AD IN THE SPORTING PRESS. IT WAS A SMALL AD AND WENT LIKE THIS "BROOD BITCH FOR SALE, GAME BALL-RAYMONDS PRIDE" BITCH HAS HAD WINNING LITTER TO CARTERS LAD" PRICE 550

PUNTS I REALISED THAT THAT WAS THE BREEDING OF MAKE HISTORY WHO HAD WON THE 1988 IRISH DERBY, MAKING THE BITCH A LITTER SISTER TO HIM. SHE'D QUALIFIED TO RACE AND ONLY HAD A COUPLE OF RACES THEN BROKE DOWN INJURED. I IMMEDIATELY PHONED THE NUMBER AND THE BITCH WAS STILL AVAILABLE AND TOLD THE MAN I WANTED HER AND WOULD COME THE NEXT MORNING

FOR HER WHICH I DID. SHE CHANGED HANDS FOR 500 PUNTS, AND I'D GOT MYSELF A LITTER SISTER TO A DERBY WINNER FOR SMALL MONEY. IT SHOWS HOW FAR BREEDING HAS PROGRESSED IN SOME WAYS WHEN YOU CONSIDER PRICES FOR BROODS HAVEN'T GONE UP IN 16 YEARS. 500 PUNTS FOR THAT BITCH WAS A BARGAIN EVEN THEN. THE MAN TOLD ME HE HADN'T HAD A SINGLE CALL FOR HER APART FROM MINE. IT DIDN'T OCCUR TO HIM TO MENTION IN THE AD THAT SHE WAS A SISTER TO MAKE HISTORY/DERBY WINNER. HER FIRST LITTER WAS TO CARTERS LAD AS MENTIONED, THEY WERE PRETTY AVERAGE. HER NEXT LITTER TO KYLE JACK WERE PRETTY MUCH ALL OPEN CLASS/TOP GRADE INCLUDING 'CENTREBACK' WINNER OF THE MIDLAND PUPPY DERBY AND 2ND IN THE LAURELS. HER NEXT LITTER TO STRANGE DILLY (MORE LATER) WERE ALL MINOR OPEN CLASS

AND THE LITTER OF 9 WON OVER 100 RACES AND INCLUDED USEFUL LATER BROODS RACEFIELD DILLY, AND KATE NO STRANGER(GRAND-DAM OF PRODUCE STAKES WINNER 'GIVE AND GO' (AT STUD). I WOULDN'T USE A BITCH THAT WAS VERY

NERVOUS OR UNDER 55LBS(PREFERABLY 58+), PEOPLE DON'T WANT TO BUY SMALL OR NERVOUS PUPS NO MATTER HOW REASONABLY PRICED THEY ARE. REMEMBER THERE ARE NO GUARANTEES WHEN IT COMES TO BREEDING, AND YOU NEED A LOT OF LUCK TO GO WITH THE RIGHT BLOOD MIX. THE ONLY THING THAT SEEMS TO BE ALWAYS CERTAIN IS THAT VERY FEW CLASSIC WINNERS ARE NOT FROM PROVEN AND CHOICELY BRED DAMS/DAMLINES. MANY PEOPLE BREED FROM A BITCH THAT THEY'VE HAD RACING FOR THEM PURELY OUT OF SENTIMENT AND WITH NO REGARD TO BLOODLINES. I BELIEVE TOO MANY GREYHOUNDS ARE BRED THIS WAY.

STUD DOGS AND THE GREATEST MYTHS IN BREEDING TODAY

MYTH 1: THE STUD FEE IS THE SMALLEST COST OF BREEDING
A LITTER.
MYTH 2: YOU NEED TO GO TO A TOP STUD DOG(and pay a big
fee) TO SELL YOUR PUPS.

FIRSTLY I'M A STUDKEEPER MYSELF WITH AUSTRALIAN STUD DOGS, ELLES DOMINATOR (LIGHT OF FIRE X ELLE SHANTY) AND TOLL SECURITY (RAPID JOURNEY-SUNSET SAVANAH), AND THE PURE IRISH BRED 'REACTABOND REBEL' (WHO HAS JUST RECENTLY WENT TO AMERICA).

THE FOLLOWING IS WHAT I BELIEVE REGARDING STUD DOGS IN GENERAL:

NO DOG CAN MAKE IT AS A SUCCESSFUL SIRE WITHOUT A DECENT NUMBER OF BITCHES, INCLUDING A DECENT AMOUNT OF QUALITY THROWN INTO THE QUANTITY. SOME STUD DOGS ARE BETTER THAN OTHERS CERTAINLY, BUT MANY DO NOT GET THE PATRONAGE TO BE FAIRLY JUDGED AGAINST OTHERS 'THAT DO', AND HOW CAN ANY 2 STUDS BE COMPARED UNLESS THEY'VE HAD THE SAME QUALITY AND NUMBER OF BITCHES, AND A SIMILAR NUMBER OF PUPS TO HAVE RACED? IT'S PRACTICALLY IMPOSSIBLE TO COMPARE ANY STUD DOG AGAINST ANOTHER, EXCEPT MAYBE THE TOP 3 OR TOP5 BECAUSE ALMOST CERTAINLY THE DOGS IN THESE POSITIONS

WILL HAVE HAD AMPLE OPPORTUNITY TO SHOW THEIR WORTH.

I GOT A STUD DOG CALLED CARDIGAN (TOP HONCHO-QUEEN PANTHER) FOR NOTHING. HE'S SUPERBLY BRED, VERY FAST(2ND ENG PUPPY DERBY), WON MANY OPENS AND EQUALLED A TR. MANY DOGS LIKE HIM ARE AVAILABLE BECAUSE THEY'RE NOT WANTED BY BREEDERS. TAKING A DOG LIKE THIS WON'T MAKE YOU ANY MONEY ON STUD FEES, BUT HE COULD BE YOUR PERSONAL STUD DOG FOR NOTHING. USE THE LIKES OF HIM ON YOUR BITCHES AND YOU CAN AFFORD TO SELL YOUR PUPS THAT BIT LOWER PRICED. DON'T JUST USE ANY DOG THAT WON OPEN RACES THOUGH. CARDIGAN WAS A TOP CLASS DOG WITH BREEDING TO MATCH. KEEP YOUR EYES AND EARS OPEN AND THIS IS WHAT YOU CAN GET FOR NOTHING. I'VE SINCE TURNED DOWN OTHER TOP CLASS DOGS ALSO DUE TO LACK

OF SPACE. REMEMBER 'CARDIGAN'S' SIRE HAS BEEN NO1 FOR THE PAST 4 YEARS. THERE IS EVERY CHANCE THAT HE AND ANY OTHER TOP CLASS SON OF HIS HAS THE SAME SIRING ABILITY PASSED ON GENETICALLY. A DOG CAN ONLY BE

LABELLED A FAILURE OR BRANDED AS A THROWER OF 'FIGHTERS' OR 'DODGE POTS' AFTER A LARGE NUMBER OF BITCHES. DOGS LIKE ENGLISH DERBY WINNER "BALLINISKA BAND" IS AN EXAMPLE, VERY GENUINE HIMSELF, FEW DOGS THREW MORE FIGHTERS. HIS GRAND-DAM WAS PURE COURSING BRED WHICH MIGHT ACCOUNT FOR THIS. MIND YOU, EVERY STUD DOG WILL THROW A PERCENTAGE OF FIGHTERS AND NON-CHASERS, THE LAW OF AVERAGES DICTATES THIS IS SO, ITS ONLY BEYOND A CERTAIN PERCENTAGE THAT THE STUD DOGS DESERVE TO BE 'LABELLED'. DON'T FORGET A DOG'S FIGHTING TENDENCIES COULD COME FROM HIS DAMLINE, IT'S

WHEN STUD-DOGS THROW A HIGH NUMBER OF FIGHTERS OR NON-CHASERS TO TOP CLASS DAMS THAT THEY PERHAPS DESERVE TO BE LABELLED.

HOW MANY SLOW DOGS, OR BOTTOM GRADERS DO THE TOP SIRES THROW FOR EVERY OPEN CLASS DOG?

I WISH I KNEW THE TRUE ANSWER, MY GUESS WOULD BE ABOUT 30.

THE BITCH IS THE MOST IMPORTANT HALF OF THE BREEDING EQUATION, SHE MUST HAVE THE GENETIC ABILITY TO PRODUCE, THEN SHE MUST BE MATED TO A SIRE THAT IS COMPATIBLE TO HER FOR THE PUPS TO BE DECENT. IF THE STUD DOG WAS THE MOST IMPORTANT PART, WHY THEN ARE THERE AS MANY DOGS THAT ONLY MAKE 100 EUROS AT GREYHOUND SALES BY THE TOP SIRES, AS THOSE SIRED BY DOGS WHO HAVE SIRED ONLY A SMALL PERCENTAGE OF BITCHES IN COMPARISON? IN 2004, ELLES DOMINATOR SIRED APPROX 10 LITTERS, TOP HONCHO THE NO1 SIRE PRODUCED OVER 200 LITTERS. SAY THERES 6 PUPS ON AVERAGE TO A LITTER, ELLES DOMINATOR COULD HAVE 60 PUPS RACING IN 2006 COMPARED TO 1200 BY TOP HONCHO. I'M NOT SAYING ELLES DOMINATOR IS AS GOOD OR BETTER A STUD DOG THAN TOP HONCHO, BUT I AM SAYING THAT I WILL NEVER KNOW DUE TO LACK OF EQUAL OPPORTUNITY.

NO-ONE WILL EVER CONVINCE ME THAT THE STUD SCENE IS NOTHING MORE THAN A NUMBERS GAME. IF THE TOP 3 OR TOP 5

SIRES ALL HAVE EQUAL NUMBERS APPROXIMATELY, YOU CAN COMPARE THEM AGAINST EACH OTHER SOMEWHAT, BUT EVEN THEN ITS ALMOST IMPOSSIBLE AS THE VARIABLES ARE ENORMOUS. VERY, VERY OCCASIONALLY A STUD DOG WILL MAKE IT ON A SMALL NUMBER OF LITTERS DUE TO EXCEPTIONAL ABILITY. THE FEW PUPS HE HAS RUNNING WILL MAKE PEOPLE SIT UP AND TAKE NOTICE. EXAMPLES OF THESE ARE BOLD WORK, SKELLIGS TIGER, SLANEYSIDE HARE(ALL FROM THE MONALEE CHAMPION SIRELINE), AND ARDFERT SEAN. ELLES DOMINATOR AND TOLL SECURITY ARE SHOWING GREAT PROMISE ALSO DUE TO SOME FLYING PUPS FROM A HANDFUL OF BITCHES. IN THE CASES OF ARDFERT SEAN AND BOLD WORK, THEY RACED AT AROUND 63-64LBS WHICH CERTAINLY DIDN'T HELP THEIR CASES. THAT'S WHY I REGARD STUD DOG TABLES AND CHARTS AS NEXT TO USELESS OR NO MORE THAN INTERESTING READING. UNTIL SOMEONE COMES UP WITH A FAIR WAY TO JUDGE STUD DOGS ON A PUP PER PUP BASIS, THE STUD CHARTS SERVE NO PURPOSE OTHER THAN TO PUSH UP STUD FEES OF THE TOP RANKED SIRES.

I WOULDN'T USE A SIRE THAT I KNEW WAS NERVOUS OR BELOW 66LBS

WEIGHT. PROSPECTIVE BUYERS WILL RARELY BUY SMALL OR NERVOUS PUPS, AND NERVY ONES ARE A NUISANCE TO HANDLE AND WORK WITH.

DISPELLING THE MYTHS

LET'S SAY, FOR EXAMPLE, I WANT TO MATE ONE OF MY BITCHES AND I DECIDE TO SPEND 1500 EUROS ON A STUD FEE. THE BITCH IS MATED ONLY ONCE (BECAUSE THE DOG IS BUSY)AND 1500 LEAVES MY POCKET WHETHER SHE HAS A LITTER OR MISSES. THE COSTS FROM NOW ON ARE THE SAME REGARDLESS WHAT STUD FEE I WOULD'VE

PAID. OR I COULD DECIDE TO USE A TOP CLASS UNPROVEN SON INSTEAD OF THE DOG @ 300 INSTEAD OF USING THE FATHER @ 1500, THAT 1200 EURO SAVING WOULD GO A LONG WAY TOWARDS COSTS FOR THE 'HOPEFULLY' FUTURE LITTER WHEN BORN IN 9 WEEKS. ADDED TO THE FACT THE SON IS CERTAIN TO BE LESS BUSY AND I COULD PROBABLY GET 2 MATINGS TO HIM INCREASING THE CHANCE OF GETTING A

LITTER, ALSO HE'S A YOUNGER DOG THAT MIGHT GIVE ME A BIGGER LITTER AS YOUTH USUALLY GOES HAND IN HAND WITH HIGH FERTILITY. BUT LET'S SAY I GO FOR THE 1500 OPTION, AND I DON'T GET A LITTER. WHAT THEN? DEPENDING ON THE RULES OF THE STUDKENNEL I MAY "ONLY" BE ELIGIBLE FOR A RETURN MATING, OR I MAY BE ABLE TO GET 80% OF MY MONEY BACK, WHICH IS 1200. THIS MEANS MY MATING WHICH PRODUCED NO PUPS HAS COST ME 300 EUROS, PLUS THE TIME AND EXPENSE INVOLVED IN GETTING HER THERE AND BACK. THERE ARE A COUPLE OF KENNELS THAT OFFER A 100% REFUND IF A BITCH MISSES, BUT MOST DON'T. IF YOU CAN ONLY GET A REPEAT MATING DUE TO NO OTHER OPTION, AS IN SOME

KENNELS, YOU MIGHT FIND THAT WHEN YOU TRY TO BOOK YOUR BITCH IN AGAIN, THAT THE DOG IS ALREADY BOOKED AND YOU CAN'T GET HIM. THIS HAPPENS OFTEN, VERY OFTEN. BELIEVE ME.

THERE ARE MANY BREEDERS I KNOW HAVE GIVEN UP THE GAME BECAUSE THEY'VE SPENT LARGE SUMS OF CASH ON STUD FEES AND

NOT GOTTEN ANY PUPS, AND THEN COULDN'T GET THEIR "FREE SERVICES" HONOURED.

TRUE STORY

A FRIEND OF MINE WHO LIVES IN NORTHERN IRELAND BOOKED A TOP STUD DOG AT A LARGE STUD KENNEL IN TIPPERARY. THE FEE WAS 1250 EUROS AT THE TIME (THE SAME DOG TODAY, IS 1500 PLUS IMPLANT COST, I DON'T THINK THEY'RE DOING NATURAL MATINGS WITH HIM ANYMORE). ANYWAY, HE SENT THE BITCH DOWN VIA GREYHOUND TRANSPORT(60 EUROS ROUND TRIP), WAS TOLD SHE WAS MATED AND SENT BACK THE FOLLOWING WEEK.

THE BITCH MISSED/NO PUPS. SOME TIME PASSED AND MY FRIEND HAD ANOTHER BITCH COME IN SEASON AND WAS ABLE TO GET HER BOOKED IN FOR HIS FREE SERVICE. SO HE SENT HER DOWN AGAIN VIA TRANSPORTER(ANOTHER 60 EUROS). TOLD SHE WAS MATED AND CAME BACK TO HIM THE FOLLOWING WEEK. THIS BITCH MISSED ALSO/NO PUPS. SOME TIME

PASSED AND THE FELLA HAD ANOTHER BITCH COME IN SEASON, HE PHONED THE STUD KENNEL AND SAID WHO HE WAS AND THE CIRCUMSTANCES REGARDING HIS STORY ETC, AND WANTED THE SAME DOG AGAIN AS HE REALLY FANCIED A LITTER FROM THIS DOG. NOW HE WASN'T ASKING FOR ANOTHER "FREE SERVICE", BUT HE EXPECTED TO BE OFFERED A REDUCTION IN PRICE. HE WAS TOLD THE DOG WAS BUSY, AND MY FRIEND INQUIRED AS TO THE AVAILABILITY OF JUST ABOUT EVERY OTHER STUD DOG IN THE KENNEL, BUT STRANGELY ENOUGH NONE OF THEM WAS AVAILABLE AND HE WAS BASICALLY TOLD HE HAD BEEN GIVEN HIS FREE SERVICE AND THAT WAS THAT. OVER 1300 EUROS SPENT AND NOTHING BUT A WASTE OF TIME. THERE OUGHT TO BE A LAW AGAINST SUCH PRACTICES AND THE ABILITY TO DO THAT AND GET AWAY WITH IT.

HOW MANY OTHERS HAS THE SAME THING HAPPENED TO IN THIS KENNEL AND IN MANY OTHERS? HOW MUCH MONEY DO CERTAIN STUDKEEPERS HAVE BELONGING TO PEOPLE WHO DIDN'T RECEIVE ANY PUPS FOR THEIR MONEY? NEEDLESS TO SAY, MY

FRIEND NEVER WENT BACK TO THAT KENNEL AGAIN.

OK, SAY THE BITCH HAS A LITTER OF PUPS, HIP HIP HOORAY!!

HOW MANY PUPS DO I NEED TO MAKE SPENDING 1500 WORTHWHILE, TAKING INTO ACCOUNT HOW MANY I WILL NEED TO SELL TO RECOUP THE STUD FEE, FOOD BILLS, BEDDING COSTS, WORMING OUT AND VACCINATIONS? I WOULD SAY SPENDING 1500 OR MORE ON A STUD FEE, ADDED TO WHICH ALL THE OTHER COSTS OUTLINED ABOVE

(WHICH ARE VERY DIFFICULT TO PUT A FIGURE ON), I WOULD NEED TO GET A BIG LITTER OF AT LEAST 8 PUPS (AND MORE DOGS THAN BITCHES) TO HAVE ANY HOPE OF BREAKING EVEN, LET ALONE MAKE A LITTLE MONEY.

OK, SAY I GET A LITTER OF 5 DOGS AND 3 BITCHES THAT SURVIVE TO 12 WEEKS (SELLING TIME). IT IS MY BROOD'S FIRST LITTER (ONE OF THE ABOVE BITCHES LISTED, SAY), SHE'S NICELY BRED, HAS RACE WINNING FORM, FROM A GOOD LITTER AND PROVEN DAMLINE. ONLY MINUS POINT IS SHE'S UNPROVEN.

HOW MUCH CAN I SELL FOR? WHAT IS THE MOST I CAN GET FOR THE 4 DOGS AND 2 BITCHES I WANT TO SELL? (ASSUMING I WANT TO KEEP 1D AND 1B FOR MYSELF) WOULD I GET 850 FOR A DOG AND 650 EUROS FOR THE BITCHES EACH? NOT A BLOODY HOPE AT TODAY'S MARKET. YOU WILL SEE PLENTY ADVERTISED AT THESE PRICES AND I DON'T THINK THEY'RE TOO DEAR, TAKING ALL THINGS INTO ACCOUNT. BUT YOU ALSO SEE THE SAME LITTERS RE-ADVERTISED OVER AND OVER AGAIN BECAUSE PEOPLE WON'T PAY THE PRICE. THE MOST I COULD CONFIDENTLY PREDICT GETTING FOR THE ABOVE SCENARIO, TO ENABLE THE PHONE TO RING AND ACTUALLY SELL!!! IS MAYBE 600 AND 400 EUROS FOR DOGS AND BITCHES RESPECTIVELY. AND I MIGHT NOT GET THAT MUCH THE WAY THINGS ARE TODAY. I WOULD HAVE TO SELL 4 DOGS AND 2 BITCHES AT THE VERY LEAST, BY MY RECKONING TO BREAK EVEN AND I MIGHT BE FOOLING MYSELF AT THAT.

NOW, SAY I USE A SIRE @ 300 ON THE SAME BITCH AND I GET A LITTER OF 8, AGAIN 5D 3B. TOP CLASS YOUNG DOG RECENTLY INTRODUCED AT STUD. WHAT

WOULD THESE PUPS REALISTICALLY SELL FOR? WELL, I CAN TELL YOU EXACTLY BECAUSE I HAVE SOLD PLENTY OF SIMILAR PUPS RECENTLY.

I MIGHT GET 450 AND 350 RESPECTIVELY, BUT I KNOW THE PHONE WOULD JUMP OUT OF MY POCKET @ 400 AND 290.

NOW, IM SURE YOU CAN WORK OUT WHICH DOG IS THE BETTER BET, NOT FORGETTING THE OBJECTIVE IS TO KEEP A DOG AND BITCH, SELL THE REST, AND HOPE TO COME OUT AT LEAST EVEN IF NOT IN FRONT.

IN TODAY'S MARKET, THE ODDS ARE DEFINITELY STACKED IN THE CHEAPER STUD DOGS FAVOUR. THE 2 STUD DOGS I PICKED FOR THE ABOVE EXAMPLES ARE TOMS LITTLE JO (TOMS THE BEST-WESTMEAD JOSIE) WHO STANDS @300 EUROS (WINNER OF 4 GROUP EVENTS AND TR 550 CLONMEL), AND HIS FATHER TOMS THE BEST WHO STANDS @1500. YET PEOPLE STILL FLOCK TO THE TOP SIRES, SWALLOWING THE HYPE OF FANCY ADVERTS AND HOPING TO SELL PUPS AT HIGH PRICES. ALL THE SIRES IN THE TOP 5 OR TOP 10 STUD CHARTS WERE ONCE UNPROVEN. DIFFERENCE IN THEM AND MOST THAT DON'T MAKE IT IS THAT THEY

HAD THE BENEFIT OF BEING IN A BIG STUD KENNEL AND POSSIBLY BENEFITTING FROM AN OVERFLOW OF BITCHES MEANT FOR OTHER PROVEN SIRES IN THE SAME KENNEL, AND OF COURSE THE BIGGER THE KENNEL THE MORE PROMOTIONALLY STRONG IT IS.

SMALL STUDKEEPERS AND BIG STUD KENNELS CAN BE LIKENED TO THE DEMISE OF THE CORNER SHOP AND THE RISE OF THE HUGE SUPERMARKETS. SUPERMARKETS ARE GETTING BIGGER AND RICHER, THE CORNER SHOPS ARE CLOSING DOWN. WHAT PEOPLE DON'T REALISE IS THAT THE BIGGER OVERHEADS ANY BUSINESS HAS, THE MORE PROFIT IT MUST MAKE, OR IT CANNOT OPERATE. IN THE STUD GAME, THE SMALLER STUDKEEPERS CAN PRICE THEIR DOGS CHEAPER

BUT SIMPLY CANNOT MATCH THE SELECTION AVAILABLE AND SPEND THE MONEY NECESSARY TO PROMOTE THEIR DOGS ON AN EQUAL BASIS. THE REVENUE COMING INTO A LEADING STUD KENNEL FROM THEIR TOP DOG ALONE PAYS THEIR BLANKET ADVERTISING COSTS IN THE GREYHOUND PAPERS. MORE AND MORE BREEDERS ARE PATRONISING PARTICULAR

KENNELS REGULARLY, IRRESPECTIVE OF BLOODLINES OR WHAT STUD-DOGS THAT KENNEL HAS. I RECKON AT LEAST 90% OF LITTERS BRED IN IRELAND TODAY ARE COMING FROM 4

STUD KENNELS. THAT'S APPROX 4000 LITTERS. EXAMPLES HERE ARE A FEW EXAMPLES OF FAMOUS IRISH DOGS, SIRES AND DAMS WHO ARE

PREDOMINANTLY LINEBRED THROUGH GENERATIONS 4,5, AND 6. THE 3RD GENERATION APPEARS IN A COUPLE OF EXAMPLES BUT NEVER DUPLICATED 3X3.

MASTER MCGRATH, FIRST IRISH DOG TO WIN THE WATERLOO CUP 3

TIMES 84% OF DIFFERENT ANCESTRY. HE HAS 5 INDIVIDUAL EXAMPLES OF LINEBREEDING. CLOSEST IS 4X5X5X6 TO KING

COB=14% OF HIS PEDIGREE.

SPANISH BATTLESHIP WINNER OF THE IRISH DERBY 3 TIMES 82% OF

DIFFERENT ANCESTRY. HE HAS 4 INDIVIDUAL EXAMPLES OF LINEBREEDING. CLOSEST IS 5X5X5X6X6X6 TO MUTTON CUTLET=14% OF HIS PEDIGREE. NEWDOWN HEATHER 84% PERCE.

THE STUD FEE IS THE BIGGEST SINGLE EXPENSE INVOLVED

IN BREEDING, IF YOU USE A SIRE IN THE HIGHER PRICE BRACKETS. LET'S NOT FORGET THAT MOST DOGS AT STUD (EXCLUDING

SOME INFERIOR IMPORTS) ARE AT STUD BECAUSE THEY

WERE VERY FAST DOGS. ALL FAST DOGS ARE CAPABLE TO A GREATER OR LESSER EXTENT OF SIRING THE SAME. DON'T BE AFRAID TO USE AN UNPROVEN DOG, ALL BREEDING IS A GAMBLE AND YOU MIGHT AS WELL GAMBLE WITH LESS MONEY THAN NECESSARY. IF NO-ONE EVER USED YOUNG, UNPROVEN DOGS, BREEDING WOULD EVENTUALLY DIE OUT. HISTORY SHOWS THAT DOGS BREED ON, NEW BLOOD REPLACES OLD.

BLOODLINES

LINEBREEDING

I'M NOT GOING TO DELVE VERY DEEPLY INTO THIS OTHER THAN SAY WHAT I, MYSELF, BELIEVE.

LATELY, THERE HAS BEEN A LOT OF TALK ABOUT LINEBREEDING, AND PARTICULARLY IN AUSTRALIA MOST OF THEIR CHAMPIONS TEND TO BE LINEBRED TO SOME DEGREE, SOME TO A REMARKABLE DEGREE!

I THINK PART OF THE REASON FOR THIS IS THAT THE PURE AUSTRALIAN BLOODLINE POOL IS QUITE SMALL AND THEREFORE LIMITED (THUS THEIR HOMEBRED CHAMPIONS CAN ONLY COME FROM SO MANY LINES).

THERE ARE MANY MORE DIFFERENT LINES IN IRISH AND AMERICAN BLOOD POOLS TO CHOOSE FROM, WHICH IS ONE REASON WHY LINEBREEDING IS MUCH LESS COMMON HERE AND AMERICA, COMPARED TO AUSTRALIA. ONE THING THAT AUSTRALIAN BREEDING HAS SHOWN US IS THAT LINEBREEDING OFTEN WORKS! I HAVE STARTED LINEBREEDING MYSELF BUT NOT TOO CLOSELY. I THINK THE CLOSER YOU LINEBREED, THE MORE RISK THERE IS IN PRODUCING A

FAULT IN THE LINE, AS WELL AS MAKING THE LINE FASTER IF THE BREEDING WORKS. I BELIEVE THAT AUSTRALIAN DOGS ARE THE FASTEST TRACK GREYHOUNDS IN THE WORLD RIGHT NOW. PART OF THIS IS

UNDOUBTEDLY DUE TO THE PRESENCE OF LINEBREEDING, WHICH I BELIEVE CAN REINFORCE A DOMINANT LINE WHICH INCREASES SPEED. THE FASTER A DOG IS THE MORE INJURY PRONE HE IS ALSO, THE FASTEST MUST SURELY BE THE MOST AT RISK?

I THINK CLOSE LINEBREEDING SOMETIMES ALSO PRODUCES UNWANTED CHARACTERISTICS LIKE FIGHTING, INJURY PRONENESS (THERE SEEMS TO BE AN AWFULLY HIGH PERCENTAGE OF YOUNG AUSTRALIAN STUD DOGS WHO RETIRED EARLY WITH LESS THAN 15 RACES BEFORE BREAKING DOWN). TOP CLASS DOGS IN IRELAND AND AMERICA BREAKDOWN TOO OF COURSE, BUT I THINK THE AVERAGE HIGH-CLASS DOG IN THESE 2 COUNTRIES HAS A LONGER RACING

CAREER IN GENERAL THAN HIS COMPARABLE AUSTRALIAN COUNTERPART DUE TO LESS LINEBREEDING IN HIS PEDIGREE.

SOME WILL ARGUE THAT OUR DOGS DON'T BREAK DOWN AS OFTEN

BECAUSE THEY'RE NOT AS FAST, AND AMERICAN DOGS WHO SEEM TO BE THE

LEAST INJURY PRONE OF ALL (MANY HAVE 3 SEASON CAREERS AND OVER 100 RACES) AND ARE THOUGHT BY MANY AUSTRALIANS AND IRISH TO BE SLOWEST OF ALL. I DON'T AGREE WITH THIS; I THINK MOST CHAMPION GREYHOUND'S WOULD BE A CHAMPION IN ANY COUNTRY.

BEFORE GREYHOUND DATA CAME ALONG IT WAS VERY UNCOMMON FOR AN IRISH BREEDER TO LOOK BEYOND 3 GENERATIONS BACK WHEN RESEARCHING A PEDIGREE (MOST WOULDN'T HAVE BEEN ABLE TO EVEN IF THEY WANTED TO). GREYHOUND-DATA ALSO GIVES US THE PERCENTAGE OF DIFFERENT ANCESTORS WITHIN ANY PEDIGREE.

WHAT AMAZES ME IS HOW MANY IRISH BRED CHAMPIONS OF OLD WERE LINEBRED TO QUITE A DEGREE!

I BET ALSO THAT THEIR BREEDERS WERE UNAWARE OF THE FACT. I FEEL LINEBREEDING FROM MY PERSPECTIVE IS SAFEST AND BEST NO CLOSER THAN WITHIN 4 GENERATIONS OF A PEDIGREE, AND I THINK THAT YOU CAN SAFELY MULTIPLY AS MANY QUALITY LINES AS YOU LIKE THROUGH THE 4TH,5TH AND 6TH GENERATION WHEN PLANNING A LITTER

WITHOUT PRODUCING DEFECTS, YET STILL BE HIGHLY

LIKELY TO INFLUENCE THEIR ABILITY TO RUN FAST. IN OTHER WORDS, I THINK LINEBREEDING SUCCESSFUL LINES THROUGH THE

4TH, 5TH, AND 6TH GENERATIONS ISN'T TOO DISTANT TO INFLUENCE A RESULTING LITTER.

NUTS AND BOLTS SECTION

HERE IS WHERE YOU WILL FIND VARIOUS WAYS AND TIPS TO CUT DOWN ON YOUR COSTS.

WORMING

WORMING COSTS ARE VERY HIGH FOR DOGS, HORSES AND CATS, COMPARED TO FARM ANIMALS LIKE SHEEP, COWS, AND PIGS.

WHY?

FARMERS HAVE HUNDREDS OF ANIMALS AND SIMPLY COULDN'T FORK OUT 3.50 EUROS PER TABLET FOR EVERY 10 KG

BODYWEIGHT (THE PRICE FOR 1 DRONTAL TABLET AT MY LOCAL VETS).

IMAGINE 100 COWS BEING WORMED, for 3.50 PER 10KG, 100 TABLETS OR MORE EACH COW! ALSO, DOG, CAT, AND HORSE OWNERS USUALLY ARE WILLING TO SPEND LOTS OF MONEY ON THEIR PET'S WELFARE. THE MORE EXPENSIVE BRANDS OF CAT FOOD AND THINGS LIKE FLEA COLLARS, ETC. COST MORE MONEY THAN THEIR EQUIVALENT DOGGY COUNTERPARTS.

WHY?

AGAIN, CAT OWNERS TYPICALLY SPEND MORE ON THEIR CAT THAN THE AVERAGE DOG OWNER SPENDS ON THEIR DOG. A FLEA COLLAR FOR A CAT CAN'T DIFFER MUCH FROM THAT FOR A DOG (AND IT'S ONLY HALF THE SIZE), YET IT CARRIES A HIGHER PRICE TAG. THEY CHARGE MORE BECAUSE THEY CAN GET AWAY WITH IT. IT ALL COMES DOWN TO MONEY AND PROFIT MAKING.

PARAZOLE PUPPY WORMER COSTS ME 9 EUROS (£6) FOR 100ML DRONTAL PUPPY WORMER IS 17 EUROS FOR 50ML BOTH DO FOR YOUNG PUPS UP TO 12 WEEKS. DRONTAL WORMING TABLETS (1 TAB PER

10KG BODYWEIGHT) ARE 3.50 EUROS EACH; ZANTAL ARE 2.30 EUROS EACH, THESE DO FOR PUPS OVER 12 WEEKS AND ALL OLDER DOGS.

I HAVE FOUND THAT THE BEST WORMER OF ALL IS PANACUR 10%. YOU CAN BUY IT FOR APPROX 50 EUROS PER LITRE, WHICH WILL EFFECTIVELY WORM OUT 40-50 DOGS OF ALL AGES AND SIZES. IT'S BEST GIVEN AS 5 ML PER 10KG BODYWEIGHT FOR 3 DAYS IN A ROW. WORMING BROODS AFTER MATING. I WOULD WORM A BITCH SHORTLY A DAY OR TWO BEFORE MATING HER, THEN FROM

SHES 6 WEEKS IN PUP I GIVE HER A DAILY DOSE OF 2.5 ML OF PANACUR PER 10KG, RIGHT UP UNTIL THE PUPS ARE OLD ENOUGH TO BE WORMED THEMSELVES. TRY THIS FOR YOURSELF AND BE AMAZED AT THE RESULTS, AND YOU'LL VIRTUALLY HAVE WORM FREE PUPS AND BROODS DURING THE MOST VULNERABLE TIMES. THE BEST THING ABOUT PANACUR IS THAT YOU CAN USE IT ON DOGS OF ALL AGES, FROM 3 WEEK OLD PUPS TO 3 YR OLD RACE DOGS. THERE'S NO FASTING NECESSARY AND THE DOGS SUFFER NO SICKNESS.

A MAN WHO OWNS A GREYHOUND SUPPLY SHOP IN IRELAND WAS SELLING DRONTAL

WORMING TABLETS FOR 2 EUROS EACH(3.50 FROM MOST VETS). YOU MUST HAVE A LICENCE TO SELL SUCH TABLETS IN IRELAND AND THIS MAN DIDN'T, SO WAS THEREFORE SELLING THEM ILLEGALLY. THE MAN SOLD HUNDREDS OF THESE TABLETS, WAS FOUND OUT, TAKEN TO COURT AND HANDED A 4 MONTH JAIL SENTENCE (WHICH I UNDERSTAND HE IS APPEALING). THE NEED FOR SUCH LICENCES AS FAR AS IM CONCERNED, EXISTS SOLELY SO THAT VETS AND PHARMACEUTICAL COMPANIES HAVE NO COMPETITION AND CAN CHARGE EXORBITANT PRICES. WHY SHOULD DOG WORMERS COST SO MUCH MORE THAN THOSE FOR OTHER ANIMALS WHEN THE INGREDIENTS IN MANY CASES ARE NO DIFFERENT?

VACCINATION COSTS

PUPS MUST BE VACCINATED, AND NOT ONLY FOR PARVO-VIRUS AS SOME DO BUT FOR DISTEMPER, HARDPAD AND MOST ESPECIALLY LEPTOSPIROSIS (JAUNDICE). THE VACCINATION DHPPI + LEPTO COVERS ALL THE ABOVE AND MORE (COMMONLY

KNOWN AS THE SEVEN-IN-ONE). I CAN BUY THIS VACCINATION COMPLETE WITH A SYRINGE AND DELIVERED TO MY DOOR FOR 8.50 EUROS (£5.65) EACH.

MY LOCAL VETS CHARGE 30 EUROS FOR THIS, ONLY DIFFERENCE I ADMINISTER IT MYSELF. THE VACCINATIONS ARE BY A LEADING PHARMACEUTICAL COMPANY. THE VACCINATION COMES COMPLETE WITH THE STICKERS FOR PROOF OF VACCINATION THAT YOU CAN STICK ONTO THE PUP'S PEDIGREE PAPER. MOST PEOPLE VACCINATE PUPS @ 6 WEEKS AND 12 WEEKS. THE WAY I DO IT IS ON THE ADVICE OF MY VET FRIEND. I VACCINATE THE MOTHER TO BE @ AT 6-7WKS OR AS SOON AS I KNOW SHES IN WHELP. THIS GIVES THE PUPS IMMUNITY THROUGH THE MOTHERS MILK RIGHT UP TO WEANING TIME. I DON'T DO THE PUPS AT 6 WEEKS, TO DO SO MY FRIEND BELIEVES WILL ONLY CANCEL OUT THE IMMUNITY THAT THE PUPS ALREADY HAVE FROM MUM. I WAIT TIL 10-11 WEEKS, HE THINKS THE LONGER TO WAIT IS BETTER AS THE OLDER THE PUPS GET, THEIR IMMUNITY STRENGTHENS AND IF THEY WERE UNFORTUNATE ENOUGH TO

CATCH SOMETHING, THE OLDER THEY ARE THE MORE

INHERENT TOOLS THEY HAVE TO FIGHT IT. SO SAY I HAVE A LITTER OF 8, I INNOCULATE WITH THE DHPPI AND THE LEPTO TOGETHER @ 10 WEEKS. 2 WEEKS LATER I GIVE THEM AN EXTRA LEPTO BOOSTER ON ITS OWN.COSTING 2.50 EUROS DELIVERED.

SO TOTAL VACCINATION COSTS ARE AS FOLLOWS:

9 X 8.50(8 PUPS PLUS MUM),=76.50 EURO,PLUS 8 X 2.50=20 EURO. TOTAL COST: 96.50 EURO(£64).

COST PER PUP IS 11 EUROS(£7) FOR 2 INJECTIONS.

IF YOU'VE EVER GOTTEN A VET TO VACCINATE YOUR LITTER YOU KNOW WHAT IT COSTS BY COMPARISON.

I HAVE WHELPED DOWN OVER 20 LITTERS FOR MYSELF AND OTHERS IN THE LAST 2 YEARS ALONE USING THE ABOVE AND HAVE HAD NO SICKNESS OR DISEASE. I WILL REVEAL MY SOURCE FOR OBTAINING THE ABOVE IF YOU EMAIL ME DIRECTLY AND ASK FOR IT.

I HAVE BEEN TOLD RECENTLY THAT NEW REGULATIONS REGARDING THE SALE OF THESE VACCINATIONS TO NON-VETERINARY PERSONNEL MAY BECOME A THING OF THE PAST. ANYTHING ANY GOOD, THE VETS USUALLY GAIN CONTROL OF IT EVENTUALLY.

BEDDING

I USE STRAW FOR BEDDING, EXCEPT WHEN WHELPING BITCHES; I USE OLD CARPET FOR THE FIRST COUPLE OF WEEKS (ANY CARPET SHOP WILL GIVE YOU REMNANTS FOR FREE). STRAW NEEDS CHANGED MORE REGULARLY THAN PAPER BEDDING BUT THE DOGS PREFER IT, AND IT'S PROBABLY WARMER FOR THEM. IT'S ALSO CHEAPER. A ROUND BALE OF STRAW COSTS ABOUT 8 EUROS AND LASTS ME ABOUT 2 MONTHS, AND PROVIDES BEDDING FOR UP TO 70 DOGS. SQUARE BALES ARE MORE EASILY HANDLED BUT MORE EXPENSIVE, YET STILL CHEAPER THAN PAPER. I USE WOOD SHAVINGS IN THE LIE-DOWN AREA OF THE DOGS BED IN THE WARM SUMMER MONTHS. YOU CAN USE WOODSHAVINGS ALL YEAR

ROUND IF YOU PUT A KENNEL COAT ON EACH DOG IN THE COLDER MONTHS AND NOT USE STRAW OR PAPER BEDDING AT ALL (OBVIOUSLY, DOESN'T APPLY TO YOUNG PUPS), AND THIS IS THE LEAST LABOUR INTENSIVE WAY OF THE LOT.

SOME PEOPLE THINK STRAW IS FULL OF FLEAS BUT FLEAS ABOUND EVERYWHERE WHERE THERE'S HEAT SO I DON'T BELIEVE THIS. ANYWAY, I WILL SHOW YOU HOW TO KEEP YOUR DOGS FREE OF FLEAS LATER. IF YOU CAN'T GET ACCESS TO STRAW READILY, INSTEAD OF BUYING PAPER BEDDING, ANY NEWSAGENTS WILL GIVE YOU YESTERDAYS NEWSPAPERS FOR FREE AND YOU CAN CRUMPLE THE PAGES UP AND MAKE YOUR OWN BEDDING. I PUT WOODSHAVINGS DOWN ON THE FLOOR WHICH I BUY AT 7 EUROS PER BALE, I'D USE ABOUT 2 BALES PER WEEK. ANY SAWMILL OR TIMBERYARD WILL GIVE YOU ALL THE SHAVINGS YOU WANT FOR FREE IF YOU BRING YOUR OWN BAGS AND FILL THEM UP YOURSELF, BUT I COULDN'T BE BOTHERED MYSELF AS I HAVEN'T THE TIME TO DO SO. THE WOODSHAVINGS KEEPS THE DOGS FEET WARM AND DRY IN COLD

WEATHER, AND ALSO SOAKS UP URINE AND KEEPS SUCH ODOURS DOWN.

FEEDING

MOST IMPORTANT OF ALL.

THE FOLLOWING APPLIES MAINLY TO FEEDING PUPS.

I FEED A COMPLETE DOG MEAL WHICH IS 28% PROTEIN WITH VITAMIN AND MINERAL LEVELS HIGHER THAN MOST OTHER MAKES OF COMPLETE FEEDS. IT CAN BE FED DRY OR SOAKED IN WATER OR MILK. I HAVE USED REDMILLS, CHAMPION, GAIN AND KASCO, I RECKON WHAT I'M USING IS SECOND TO NONE. THE FEED IS ESPECIALLY FOR GREYHOUNDS AND IS MANUFACTURED BY IRISHDOGFOODS (CAN BE FOUND AT irishdogfoods.com TEL 045 872701 ((ASK FOR UNA)) OR 0035345872701 FROM UK).

THE PRICE VARIES ACCORDING TO THE QUANTITY YOU BUY BUT IT'S AT LEAST 30% CHEAPER NO MATTER HOW YOU BUY IT COMPARED TO ANYTHING SIMILAR ON THE MARKET. YOU CAN BUY IT FOR AROUND 10 EUROS PER BAG IF YOU BUY A PALLET. I FEED MY PUPS THIS ADLIB.

THEY ALSO GET ABOUT A PINT OF POWDERED MILK EACH PER DAY UP TO 6 MONTHS. I GET RAW MEAT FROM A LOCAL SLAUGHTERHOUSE (THE PARTS THAT DON'T SELL SUCH AS HEAD BEEF, HEARTS, LUNGS, LIVER, KIDNEYS, AND SHEEP AND BEEF TRIPE). THIS I GET FOR NOTHING BUT THERE IS LABOUR INVOLVED IN CUTTING IT UP(NOT THE NICEST OF JOBS BUT THE PUPS LOVE IT). FOR YOUNG PUPS, I WOULDN'T GIVE THEM ANY MEAT UNTIL 6 WEEKS OLD AND NOT

COMPLETELY RAW, I'D STEEP IT FIRST IN BOILING WATER UNTIL 12 WEEKS OLD. OBVIOUSLY, YOU MUST BE VIGILANT WHEN FEEDING YOUNG PUPS, IF IT SCOURS THEM, TAKE IT AWAY AND JUST FEED THE MEAL, ETC. OF COURSE, YOU COULD COOK THE MEAT IF YOU HAVE THE TIME FOR YOUNG PUPS, BUT I FIND SOAKING IT IN SCALDING WATER GIVES AN EFFECT SIMILAR TO BOILING AND IT'S A LOT QUICKER. I ALSO BUY QUALITY MINCED BEEF AND TRIPE FOR RACING DOGS AND SCHOOLING PUPS, AT AROUND 50 CENTS PER POUND. ALSO, WATCH FOR FIGHTING (ONLY APPLIES TO PUPS USUALLY FROM 5-6 MONTHS UPWARDS); DOGS ARE CARNIVORES AND

PREFER MEAT TO ANYTHING ELSE, CUTTING THE ABOVE INTO CHUNKS AND WATCHING A LITTER COMPETE FOR THEIR SHARE IS A GOOD

SIMULATION OF HOW THEY'D REACT IN THE WILD, AND BENEFICIAL TO THEIR UPBRINGING AND DEVELOPMENT. THAT'S WHY FOR OLDER PUPS AND ADULT DOGS I GIVE IT TO THEM RAW. IT WON'T BE PRACTICAL FOR MOST PEOPLE TO GO TO SLAUGHTERHOUSES BUT YOUR LOCAL BUTCHER WILL PROVIDE YOU WITH THE ABOVE OR SIMILAR FOR LITTLE OR NOTHING IF YOU TELL HIM WHAT IT'S FOR. HE MAY EVEN BE GLAD FOR YOU TO TAKE IT OFF HIS HANDS. IF YOU'RE JUST DOING ONE LITTER AT A TIME, YOU SHOULD BE ABLE TO GET PLENTY OF FREE STUFF FOR THEM. MEAT FAT IS VERY GOOD FOR GREYHOUNDS, PARTICULARLY GROWING PUPS AND BROOD BITCHES CARRYING PUPS. MANY TRAINERS THINK FAT IS DETRIMENTAL TO RACE DOGS BUT I THINK A CERTAIN AMOUNT OF FAT DOESN'T DO ANY HARM WHATSOEVER AND IS PROBABLY BETTER GIVEN THAN NOT.

TRIPE IS A SUPERFOOD FOR GROWING PUPS IN PARTICULAR AND FULL OF FAT, IT

PUTS A GREAT BACK ON THEM. ANY MEAT I FEED IS FRESH AND FROM LOCAL, KNOWN SOURCES. I USE THE 'VOLAC' BRAND OF POWDERED MILK WHICH IS DEARER THAN SOME AT 36

EUROS (£24) 20KG BAG BUT IT'S GOOD STUFF, THE PUPS LOVE IT AND A BAG WILL LAST A LITTER OF PUPS TO 12 WEEKS. IT'S A MILK POWDER MADE FOR CALVES. DON'T MAKE IT TOO RICH THOUGH OR IT WILL SCOUR THEM.

THE LAMB EQUIVALENT 'LAMLAC' IS ALSO VERY GOOD BUT WORKS OUT QUITE A BIT MORE EXPENSIVE PER KG. IF YOU'RE ONLY DOING ONE LITTER AT A TIME, I THINK THE LAMLAC OR ANY LAMBS MILK POWDER WOULD BE MY FIRST PREFERENCE. MOST OF THESE MILK POWDERS SEEM TO BE AROUND 23% PROTEIN. I AM ALSO A GREAT BELIEVER IN RAW EGGS FOR GREYHOUNDS OF ALL AGES, BUT

ESPECIALLY FOR PUPS MIXED WITH THE WARM POWDERED MILK IS A GREAT WEANING FOOD AND BUILDS THEM UP. IT'S POSSIBLE TO GET EGGS VERY CHEAPLY, SOMETIMES FREE, FROM EGG FACTORIES WHEN THEY REMOVE THE EGGS ON SALE FROM SHOPS AND SUPERMARKETS. THESE

EGGS WILL STILL HAVE USUALLY A DAY OR TWO'S DATE STILL ON THEM SO THEY'RE PERFECTLY FRESH, AND EVEN A WEEK PAST THEIR DATE IS FINE TO USE. FAILING THIS THE CHEAPEST EGGS IN THE SUPERMARKETS ARE QUITE REASONABLE AND WELL WORTH BUYING, EGGS ARE HARD TO BEAT AS GREYHOUND FOOD FOR ALL

AGES.

I DON'T RECOMMEND FEEDING PUPS SCRAPS FROM RESTAURANT KITCHENS WHICH MANY REARERS IN IRELAND DO. SOMETIMES THE FOOD IS GOOD AND FRESH, SOMETIMES IT ISN'T AND PERSONALLY I

WOULDN'T USE IT. YOU DONT KNOW WHAT YOU'RE GETTING AND QUITE A LOT OF TENDS TO BE OFF. NEITHER WOULD I FEED STALE BAKERY BREAD WHICH CAN BE BOUGHT VERY CHEAPLY. I DON'T FEED ANY BREAD TO GREYHOUNDS WHATSOEVER. I USED TO MIX BREAD WITH THE MEAL BUT THE MEAL HAS SO MUCH MORE VITAMINS AND NUTRIENTS. I COULD SAVE QUITE A BIT OF MONEY ON MEAL COST BY DOING SO, BUT THERE'S NOTHING IN BREAD THAT THEY'RE NOT GETTING FROM MEAL NUTS.

THE PROOF IS IN THE PUDDING AS THE SAYING GOES, AND IM PROUD OF THE QUALITY OF PUPS I TURN OUT.

RINGWORM

JUST A QUICK WORD ON RINGWORM, MOST LARGE KENNELS WILL GET IT AT ONE TIME OR ANOTHER AND IT CAN SPREAD LIKE WILDFIRE. HUMANS CAN GET IT TOO AND HORSES ARE PROBABLY THE BIGGEST CARRIERS OF IT. GREYHOUNDS ARE VERY LIKELY TO PICK IT UP FROM OTHER DOGS AT THE TRACKS, SAME AS KENNEL COUGH. THERE USED TO BE A POWDER MADE FOR HORSES BUT WORKED JUST AS WELL FOR GREYHOUNDS, THAT YOU PUT INTO THE FEED BUT ITS GONE OFF THE MARKET NOW. IF THE RINGWORM ISN'T TOO BAD, MIXING A SOLUTION OF 1 PART BLEACH TO 4 PARTS WATER AND BATHING THE AFFECTED AREAS 2-3 TIMES A DAY OFTEN WILL TAKE IT AWAY. OTHER THAN THAT, THE ONLY THING AVAILABLE CURRENTLY FROM THE VET IS AN INJECTION (OF COURSE 1 PER DOG AND A VISIT TO THE SURGERY, OR CALL THE VET OUT IF YOU HAVE A FEW).

THIS OPTION, OF COURSE, IS MUCH MORE EXPENSIVE THAN THE POWDER PREVIOUSLY AVAILABLE THAT WORKED VERY WELL.

EVERY YEAR THERE SEEMS TO BE LESS AND LESS 'OVER THE COUNTER' MEDICATIONS THAT VETERINARY SHOPS WILL SELL YOU.

WOULD MONEY HAVE ANYTHING TO DO WITH IT? I WONDER.

FLEA CONTROL

FLEAS ARE THE SCOURGE OF ANY KENNEL AND MUST BE KEPT AT BAY. THERE USED TO BE A PRODUCT CALLED TICKSOL WHICH WAS A CONCENTRATE WHEN MIXED WITH WATER WOULD CLEANSE THE DOG WITH FLEAS VERY QUICKLY AND EFFICIENTLY. IT ALSO WORKED FOR TICKS (HENCE THE NAME) AND MANGE AND WAS SOLD FOR USE

ON SHEEP, CATTLE, AND PIGS (SOUNDS A BIT LIKE OUR WORMERS), BUT IT WORKED. WELL, ON GREYHOUNDS IF YOU DIDN'T MAKE IT TOO STRONG. IT WASN'T CHEAP BUT WORKED OUT REASONABLE ENOUGH. IT'S GONE OFF THE MARKET NOW. I HAVE USED SHEEP DIP WHICH COST ME 70

EUROS AND WASHED ABOUT 45 ADULT DOGS, NOT BAD BUT LABOUR INTENSIVE AND STILL NOT CHEAP. ASK YOUR LOCAL VET WHAT HE RECOMMENDS FOR FLEAS AND HE'LL PROBABLY TRY

TO SELL YOU A WASH CALLED FRONTLINE (COSTS ABOUT 24 EUROS AND WILL ONLY WASH 3-4 ADULT GREYHOUNDS), OR HE'LL RECOMMEND A 'SPOT ON' TYPE VIAL (STRONGHOLD COSTS ABOUT 10 EURO EACH DOG). NONE OF THESE ARE PRACTICAL OR AFFORDABLE IF, LIKE ME, YOU WANT TO COVER 50+ DOGS. FURTHERMORE, GETTING RID OF THE FLEAS ON A DOG IS ONE THING, ONCE YOU DO

YOU ALSO NEED TO EITHER WASH FREQUENTLY OR USE A FLEA COLLAR OR THE FLEAS COME BACK AGAIN QUICKLY.

WHAT IS THE SOLUTION?

THERE IS A GARDEN INSECTICIDE (USED COMMONLY FOR ROSES) CALLED' MALATHION LIQUID'. A 100ML BOTTLE OF THIS COSTS 8.50 EURO AND WILL WASH APPROX 90 ADULT SIZED GREYHOUNDS WHEN MIXED CORRECTLY WITH WATER. IT DOES THE DOGS COATS NO HARM WHEN

MIXED AS DIRECTED (ONE CAPFUL PER 2.5 LITRES OF WATER) AND FLEAS HATE IT AND PISS OFF INSTANTLY UPON CONTACT. IT ALSO TAKES CARE OF TICKS. No Longer available.

IN CHARLIE LISTER'S RECENT BOOK, HE RECOMMENDS A PRODUCT CALLED "DURAMITEX" WHICH IS COMMONLY USED FOR SPRAYING PIGEON LOFTS AGAINST FLEAS. THE MAIN INGREDIENT CONTAINED IN THIS IS THE SAME AS THE 'MALATHION LIQUID' (WHICH IS MUCH CHEAPER, AND AVAILABLE FROM ANY GOOD GARDEN CENTRE). THE WAY I USE THE MALATHION LIQUID IS MIXED AS DESCRIBED ABOVE AND PUT INTO A ONE LITRE SPRAY CONTAINER THAT YOU'D USE FOR SPRAYING PLANTS WITH (COST ABOUT 2.99), AND I GIVE EACH DOG A QUICK SPRAY ALL OVER WITH IT AND RUN A FLEA COMB AND GROOMING BRUSH OVER THE DOG AFTERWARDS, WHICH WORKS THE

LIQUID IN AND DRIES THE DOG OFF AS WELL AS SORTING ANY FLEAS.TAKES 5-10 MINS PER DOG.

DOING THIS DAILY IN SUMMER AND 3 TIMES A WEEK IN WINTER WILL KEEP YOUR DOGS FREE OF FLEAS AND TICKS. IT ALSO

KEEPS THE DOG LOOKING GOOD AND TAKES DEAD HAIR OUT OF HIS COAT. IT'S QUICK, IT'S EASY AND THE DOG WILL APPRECIATE THE TIME YOU SPEND ON

HIM/HER. BEFORE THIS, I USED EXPENSIVE FLEA COLLARS WHICH AREN'T THAT EFFECTIVE AFTER A MONTH OR SO @ 9 EUROS EACH. VERY EXPENSIVE WHEN MULTIPLIED BY 40 OR 50.

ADVERTISING YOUR PUPS.

OK, ASSUMING YOUR PUPS ARE COMING UP TO 12 WEEKS OR SO AND YOU WANT TO ADVERTISE THEM. NATURALLY THE LESS YOU SPEND ON ADVERTISING THE BETTER, AS IT CAN COST A FORTUNE. I HAVE SOLD DOZENS OF PUPS THIS YEAR AND SPENT VERY VERY LITTLE MONEY ADVERTISING THEM. I'VE SOLD PUPS TO IRELAND, ENGLAND, SCOTLAND AND USA.

HERE IS HOW I DO IT

ADVERTISE THEM ON GREYHOUND-DATA.COM FOR FREE. YOU CAN EVEN UPLOAD A PHOTO IN YOUR AD FOR FREE

(PICTURE ADS ARE SHOWN FIRST, AND WILL MAKE A BIG DIFFERENCE TO SELLING YOUR PUPS). THERE'S NO LIMIT TO THE NUMBER OF WORDS YOU USE EITHER, SO DESCRIBE YOUR PUPS PEDIGREES IN DETAIL. GLOBAL GREYHOUNDS CLASSIFIEDS ALSO WORKS VERY WELL; NOT FREE BUT CHEAP AT 15 DOLLARS PER AD. THERE IS ALSO THE OPPORTUNITY TO INCLUDE A PHOTOGRAPH. APART FROM ADVERTISING, THIS SITE IS THE BEST SOURCE OF GREYHOUND INFO ON THE NET. IRELANDS GREYHOUND WEEKLY, AGAIN, FREE ADVERTISING WITH NO LIMIT ON

WORDAGE USED. ALTHOUGH HUGELY WORDED ADS WILL RESULT IN SMALLER WORD PRINT, SO DON'T MAKE IT TOO WORDY. THIS PAPER IS BRILLIANT FOR SELLING, EVERY BIT AS GOOD AS THE SPORTING PRESS (WHICH COSTS A FORTUNE, LIKE FOR LIKE). USE ALL THREE OF THE ABOVE FOR A TOTAL OF 15 DOLLARS, BRILLIANT VALUE.

OTHER AVENUES

SPORTING PRESS - TOO EXPENSIVE AND DIFFICULT TO DEAL WITH IN MY EXPERIENCE GREYHOUND STAR- VERY EXPENSIVE, ONLY OF USE REALLY FOR ENGLISH BUYERS RACING POST -MOST EXPENSIVE OF ALL BUT GOOD TO ADVERTISE IN IF YOU WANT TO SPEND THE MONEY.

I DON'T USE ANY OF THE ABOVE 3. MOST IMPORTANT THING IS THIS IF YOU ASK TOO MUCH IN TODAY'S MARKET YOU WON'T SELL. IT'S A BUYERS MARKET FOR SURE AND YOU SHOULD BE AIMING TO TURN OUT FINE PUPS WHICH WANT FOR NOTHING AT THE LOWEST COST TO YOURSELF AS POSSIBLE. OTHERWISE, YOU CAN'T COMPETE WITH OTHERS (LIKE ME). THE RULES HAVE CHANGED AND YOU MUST ADAPT.

SUMMING UP.

MY PUPS ARE WELL-FED, WELL-BEDDED, THEY'RE HANDLED WELL, THEY'RE CLEAN AND DRY AND MOST IMPORTANTLY, THEY'RE CONTENT. THIS IS THE OBJECTIVE I FEEL, IF YOU HAVE A LITTER OF NICE LOOKING,

CONTENTED PUPS YOU'RE NOT DOING A WHOLE LOT WRONG, AND IF YOU PRICE THEM RIGHT, ADVERTISE THEM RIGHT, AND CUT UNNECESSARY COSTS, YOU'LL COME OUT OK AND YOU'LL BE DOING THEM BETTER THAN MOST.

THANKS,

MARK TELFORD

THIS EBOOK MAY NOT BE QUOTED, COPIED, OR EMAILED WITHOUT PERMISSION FROM THE AUTHOR.

Printed in Great Britain
by Amazon